"If you are living the single life and sex on the spectrum always has baffled you, this is the book to grab. I couldn't put it down once I started. Artemisia is such a wise woman and I love her honesty and perseverance, not to mention the 106 important rules. Read this book and learn from one of the best. This is truly a brilliant piece of work."

—*Anne Skov Jensen, Founder/Coach, A-Team Denmark, speaker*

"Artemisia states she is a modern-day feminist and she lives up to that throughout the book. Outspoken, straightforward, clever, witty and most importantly HONEST. Artemisia says it as it is and addresses topics that have been neglected or ignored in the past. The book is imaginative and engaging. I just love the 'Rules' that she has added to each chapter; so much wisdom that could easily be applied to all single women, regardless of whether or not they are on the spectrum."

—*Maxine Aston, couple counsellor, trainer and author, specialising in Asperger syndrome of related interest*

The A to Z of ASDs
Aunt Aspie's Guide to Life
Rudy Simone
Foreword by Stephen M. Shore
ISBN 978 1 78592 113 1
eISBN 978 1 78450 377 2

22 Things a Woman with Asperger's Syndrome
Wants Her Partner to Know
Rudy Simone
Illustrated by Emma Rios
ISBN 978 1 84905 883 4
eISBN 978 0 85700 586 1

Aspergirls
Empowering Females with Asperger Syndrome
Rudy Simone
ISBN 978 1 84905 826 1
eISBN 978 0 85700 289 1

22 Things a Woman Must Know If She Loves
a Man with Asperger's Syndrome
Rudy Simone
ISBN 978 1 84905 803 2
eISBN 978 1 84642 945 3

SEX AND THE
SINGLE ASPIE

ARTEMISIA

Jessica Kingsley *Publishers*
London and Philadelphia

First published in 2018
by Jessica Kingsley Publishers
73 Collier Street
London N1 9BE, UK
and
400 Market Street, Suite 400
Philadelphia, PA 19106, USA

www.jkp.com

Copyright © Artemisia 2018
Front cover image source © Panos Kefalos

Library of Congress Cataloging in Publication Data
A CIP catalog record for this book is available from the Library of Congress

British Library Cataloguing in Publication Data
A CIP catalogue record for this book is available from the British Library

ISBN 978 1 78592 530 6
eISBN 978 1 78450 918 7

Printed and bound in Great Britain

CONTENTS

INTRODUCTION

I am a modern feminist, one who embraces sexuality. I have no quarrel with the biological differences between man and woman. What I do have a problem with are manmade constructs designed to keep both genders in gilded cages that cause mental injury.

Although this is a book about a woman seeking to have and understand heterosexual relationships, I am a great fan of women. When we band together and support each other, great things can happen. Men realize there is no keeping the status quo of dominance (and sometimes bullying) when this happens. It is when we sabotage each others' efforts that we weaken ourselves as individuals and as a whole. We often do that in competition, to be seen as cool and desirable, to keep the peace, to assuage fragile egos. But it is the women who won't be bullied or dominated, who don't cry over men, that get the most out of life and love.

This book *will* be controversial. Most books about the autism spectrum are about children. We are only children for a few years. We are adults for the rest of our lives. Girls who are too young should not read this book. I would recommend over 21, depending on maturity level. Sex on the autism spectrum has always been a secret, taboo subject, as if we are not capable of having healthy sexual appetites. Rather, the topic comes up in terms of aberration, masturbation or, at best, how to have a healthy traditional relationship. But people on the spectrum have as varied a sexual life as anyone. And women talking about sexuality has always been seen as something of a threat. I have a whole chapter devoted to penises. Why not? Penises are important. No one ever speaks about them in polite society, yet, when I went to a museum recently, I counted 42 of them on the ground floor alone, carved in marble on display for all to see. I do not care about polite when I write. I care about *truth*. Only through honesty and truth do we evolve as a person, couple, or species, in a healthy direction.

We expect our writers and leaders to 'have it all.' By sharing my own fictionalized personal journeys and pitfalls, I shatter that illusion at my own expense. No one has it all. It is a myth. Despite achievements, I too am on the spectrum and, like you (or someone you know), my challenges never really leave me. They merely morph into more sophisticated ones. Please be as patient with me as I would be with you. I will openly talk about my experiences in this book. I have tried to protect everyone's identity as best I can—places, names and circumstances have been changed.

Please also try not to be judgmental. *This is not, by any means, a how-to book.* In fact, it is much more like a how not to. In my almost eternal naivete, I put myself at great risk writing this book. While some of us have good instincts, we may not act on them. Others do not have good instincts, but either way, there is no such thing as infallibility. Bad things can and do happen to women in and out of sexually charged situations. Please dear reader, dear sister on the spectrum, bear this in mind while reading. As one woman said, "We are not all as strong as you, Artemisia." Nor are very many as reckless as I can be in the pursuit of knowledge. And I suppose luck, or whatever you want to call it, was on my side. I want you to remember this if you feel at any point like I'm saying, "Be like me."

While I'm pro-sex, pro-self-actualization and whatever that means to you (as I will state later more than once), having a loving relationship with yourself is paramount. Only then do you find true joy and, once found, you will need less affirmation from others.

My gay friends: I have no idea what it's like to be a single lesbian anywhere so please understand, I cannot write that book for you. Most of us are a bit sexually flexible and have had same sex experiences, but that does not make us lesbian, any more than being shy makes someone an Aspie. The same goes for those of you who are not interested in sex, or those whose tastes and appetites are not explicitly covered in this book. This is not a clinical encyclopedia, but an epic adventure covering a lot of territory, much of it in the soul and mind as much as the body. I think it is the thoughts and emotions that will make it universal.

Love, and the seeking of it, has built and destroyed entire empires and individual souls; it is the engine that drives creation. It is the cause of all our saddest songs and most tragic tales, and our moments of greatest bliss. Without it we wither and die, internally if not literally, and to avoid this we will overturn any obstacle in our way to acquire and achieve it. We lose our cool, our dignity and sometimes all our worldly possessions and minds over this thing called Love and its twin sister, Sex.

SAFETY NOTES

- Always listen to your gut instinct—if someone makes you feel uncomfortable or threatened, or even if you feel like there's something 'not quite right' about them, avoid being alone with them. If you don't trust your own instincts, ask a trusted friend to help you evaluate.

- If you're meeting a new person, always let a friend know when and where you'll be going—if possible, try to give them the exact location and the name of the person you'll be meeting. There are lots of free apps you can download on your phone if you want to allow your friends to see your whereabouts on these outings, or if you want to be able to send an alert to local authorities quickly and discreetly. Popular choices include Circle of 6, bSafe and Watch Over Me.

- If you're unsure whether a situation is sexually-charged or platonic, don't be afraid to ask the other person. Communication is important, and as long as you're respectful you have nothing to worry about. Don't assume or guess the other person's feelings.

- Practicing safe sex ensures that you and your partner are protected against STDs when you have sex. Vaginal, oral and anal sex can all spread STDs, as all sexual fluids (semen, pre-ejaculation and vaginal fluids) can carry infections. It's important to get tested for STDs regularly. People who have any kind of sex should be tested for certain common STDs about once a year. Until you are in a mutually-committed relationship, and have both been tested, always use contraception such as condoms.

- Avoid drinking too much alcohol or taking other drugs on dates, as this blurs your judgment of situations. It also makes it harder to remember safe sex basics.

- You should trust and communicate with your partner—you should feel comfortable talking to them about safe sex. If your partner refuses to use protection or get tested, this is a sign that the partnership is not healthy.

- Both partners need to consent to a sexual relationship, and both have the ability to withdraw consent and say "no" at any point.

- Respecting your partner and potential partners is key, and you should both communicate your boundaries.

- There are no concrete rules to dating/relationships that all neurotypical people are following. The most important thing is that you feel happy, safe and respected.

CHAPTER 1

A TALE OF TWO CITIES

She sat on a bed in a shitty little flat in Greece. This was not the Kallithea she saw images of on Google. This was a neighborhood in Athens, away from the tourists, the city center and the Acropolis. Nowhere near the sea.

She had only come for five days; to get away from him, to give him time with his son. So he could sleep with other women, as he chronically seemed to need to.

The rain poured down hard outside, on her balcony overlooking nothing. She went for a walk, ate souvlaki and donuts, things that could hurt her. She didn't care. They were delicious.

"Do you know an apartment I could rent for a month?" she asked someone. She found one on Airbnb. She wasn't going back.

She didn't feel like herself. She didn't cry, she didn't hesitate, she didn't feel sad. Yet. She just knew that the narcissist was killing her and she was done.

She had been, like many Aspies, alone for much of her life. When this very handsome man had reached out to her from across the sea, on some level she hadn't trusted it. When he told her he loved her before they'd even met, her instinct was to tell him not to come. But she listened instead to others, and to her loneliness.

A year later, she knew it was time to trust her instincts. The fairy tale had simply been Grimm.

But she was worried. If she didn't have a 'boyfriend' then she couldn't have a regular sex life, could she? And, as a 'not young' woman, what chance did she have of getting one of those?

Women have had their sexuality controlled, dimmed, downplayed and in some instances vilified in most societies and throughout most of recorded history. Why was a man 'a player' and a woman 'promiscuous'? Why could men sow their wild oats, while women must wait? She had left a bad man, so why should she have to pay the price: pine and be lonely, hoping that the next one would be a knight in shining armor, instead of a douchebag in tinfoil? No, *she* would be the one to say what was right for her. Not the media, not religion, not her family, not her readers. Nobody but her.

But, the catch was, Aspergirls are naive creatures.[1] Sheep that the wolves want to devour. How could she do this, have what she wanted, and not lose her soul, mind, dignity and character? Could she channel this bookish intelligence to get what she wanted? She knew about emotional intelligence, but what about sexual intelligence, romantic intelligence? These were very different things. It was time, now, to find out exactly who she was and what she was made of.

---

1   Aspergirls is a term coined by author Rudy Simone in her book of the same name to denote females with Asperger syndrome.

CHAPTER 2

HER BIG FAT GREEK WEEKEND

She was still in Athens, in the Plaka, near Acropolis. She purposely missed her plane back. The reality of what she'd done hit her and she now missed him terribly. But, no regrets, he was bad for her. As she'd only planned to stay for five days, she'd brought only a small overnight bag of clothes with her. It was cold, shockingly so, and it rained more than she would have imagined possible. She didn't know exactly what was happening to her; she was a bit ill, quite ill actually, and was sleeping a lot.

Since she arrived in this ancient city, every morning when she awoke she would hear a truth as soon as she opened her eyes, sometimes before. A truth she knew she must act on; it was strangely reassuring. But most of the time, she felt lonely and frightened. She was grateful for her girlfriends, who rallied around her via the internet. She was their leader, or was supposed to be. She knew that showing such vulnerability would make them all lose faith in her but she was desperate. We will do anything to stay alive.

She managed to make it down the stairs needing food and medicine, and wandered into the nearest café. It was a modern-looking place, unlike most around there, with old time American jazz playing on the sound system and a cozy fireplace at one end. You could smoke inside, something even Paris didn't allow anymore. She felt exposed, as if everyone would be able to tell that she was displaced, some sort of refugee. And really, she was.

A handsome and sympathetic looking waiter approached her table. Besides taking her order, he asked where she was from.

Women with Aspergers are in many ways, like children, like little girls. The same way a child might blurt out a non sequitur, apropos of nothing, so could they. Instead of simply saying, "New York," she told him, "I've left my boyfriend in Paris and I'm not going back."

He sat down—something she'd not seen a waiter do before—looked her in the eye, and said, "Love does not make the eyes to cry. Love makes us feel good."

He was perceptive...and handsome. To her mind, he looked like a character in the film *300*. He was kind. He spoke to her. In Aspie terms, that's practically a relationship. Okay, not quite, but she was immediately infatuated.

She returned to that café twice a day when she was well enough. It was easy. They had the best lattes in the world, cheap, and the waiter, Sethos, gave her discounts on everything she ordered, with extras thrown in. He flirted, he touched her shoulders, looked her in the eyes. He wanted her, she could tell. She was desperate to get her ex out of her system. It was making her crazy, along with the souvlaki and baklava she was stuffing down her throat after two years of being gluten-free.

"Are you married?" she asked him the third time they'd met.

"Yes."

Oh. She hadn't looked at his hands for a ring. She never remembered to do that. She'd never been with a married man and was ethically opposed to it.

Still, she couldn't stop trying to be alone with him. She wanted him. She gave him her address which was only 50 metres away, he gave her his number.

She called him, and he came to her apartment that day after work. He kissed her—first her mouth and then her breasts. She was struck by the childish way he suckled on them. She didn't like it.

Thankfully he soon stopped, saying, "I have never cheated on my wife."

Artemisia was, essentially, a good person. As it turned out, she would not—could not—seduce a married man. Women in her recent past hadn't cared if they hurt her to get a night with her lover, but she was not that kind of woman. She didn't like to hurt innocent people and she was not a home-wrecker. Somewhere out there was a faithful wife, innocent and unsuspecting. She told him to leave and he did, glad to be relieved of his duty to this mutual obsession.

She sat on her balcony and stared at majestic Acropolis for a few moments before the cold drove her indoors. The mountain had such a presence—even the Nazis had conducted secret investigations to try and discover the source of its power. She could not see Parthenon from here, only one column far to the left, but she had a wonderful view of the large grotto carved into the side of the mountain. It looked like a doorway, like maybe once there was a secret entrance from there, to the temples at the top. She must look into it.

This being 'single but sexual' was going to be more complicated than she thought. Her naivete once again took her by surprise, and so did her tendency to obsess. It would take weeks for her infatuation for him to cool.

I must have some rules for myself if I'm going to survive out here, she thought.

She started with this:

. . . .

RULE #1 When you meet someone new, you are seeing only the book cover. You have no idea how many characters are in their story, and what roles they play.

. . . .

She didn't want to be the villain in any tale.

CHAPTER 3

ASCLEPIUS

She slept for 16 hours. That was not normal. She forced herself awake and Googled 'Athens' and 'sleep.' Immediately she found an entry in English which stated that a Sleeping Temple had been discovered on the slopes of Acropolis just a year and a half before. An *Asclepion*, so named for the doctor who invented them. Sleep was part of Asclepius' prescription for whatever ailed a person, whether it was emotional or physical. One had been unearthed and was on display, just half a kilometre away.

It was a bright sunny day, not too cold. As she stood in line to buy entry into the ancient temples, theatres and paths of Acropolis, she heard someone call her name. A dog ran past in response, one of many animals—although mostly cats— that lived on Acropolis. It seemed like an omen that one bore her rather unusual name, like she was meant to be there.

She was still unwell: the diverticulitis and the hemorrhaging that almost killed her a few years before had returned in full force and, although she was doing what she needed to get better, it would take time. She trudged slowly along the white gravel path, past the Dionysus theatre, until she found it. An installment of strangely new-looking marble pillars, walls and things that looked like sarcophagi clustered together between the path and the sheer face of the cliff. Parthenon was a long way ahead and above. She'd just rest here for a while. She couldn't stand. She sat on the little tributary of path that led up to the Asclepion. She wanted to lie down. More than anything in the world, she wanted to climb under the rope that kept out climbing children and smoking adults from quickly wearing down that which thousands of years of being buried in nature had preserved. She wanted to climb into that bower, behind the cool marble sarcophagus, under the shade of that tree, and sleep, knowing she was watched over by both Asclepius and Athena herself.

She laid semi-reclined on that path for an hour, propped up on one elbow, trying to look casual for the tourists that straggled past. When she finally stood it was clear that she would not make it to the top that day to see Parthenon up close. She would have to try again another day.

She went home and that night had a dream. She was on a hilltop in an open temple, watching women dance a strange and unusual dance. There was a breeze coming through the columns and she could see a starlit sky beyond the torchlight. When she woke, she had a strong sensation that she had been on a journey.

She returned to Acropolis. She kicked off her shoes and trod the path, determined to make it all the way. She got yelled at by security, several times, to put her shoes back on. She would, and then she'd kick them off again, ten steps later. The marble was slippery under shoes, but felt delicious, smooth and cool under bare feet. She noticed that there were no bird droppings to step over and no birds flying overhead.

She had also noticed from her balcony that they seemed to always fly near Acropolis but never directly over it.

She made it to the top. It was cold and windy, the sky a raw blue. The temples were roped off, including the Erecthion, the iconic temple with columns carved like women, so that one could not get close much less enter. But that was okay. Whatever was here that held power was not to be found in some temple ruin, visible to the naked eye. It was on the other side of some invisible curtain, she was sure of it.

It took weeks to heal, but slowly she began to improve. She got the things she needed from the pharmacy downstairs, bought herself a long warm sweater and began taking long daily walks around the base of Acropolis, where the streets were as narrow as tenement hallways and the air was fresh and pure.

She lived like a priestess, walking, writing and rehearsing in her apartment, providing counsel to men and women around the world via her aged laptop. Too much like her new hero, Athena, for the goddess was a renowned virgin. Despite her desire to leave the past behind, she hadn't met anyone new yet. She had an easy time meeting people, but she didn't really know how to go about meeting the right people. She tended to meet only those who sought her out, or those whom fate threw in her path—the ones that came to mow the lawn, street musicians, etc. The 'friend income' of the self-employed Aspie can be a bit slim.

Despite all her books and years, she still couldn't quite figure out men. Greek, American, Italian, or French, it didn't matter, they were all a bit of a mystery to her. Either they were a bit shy in the flirt department or she was just not to their taste. Or vice versa. So, despite having decent looks, a good heart and success, she had been single most of her adult life. Artemisia was sick to death of it and determined to change things.

She had never wanted another man to touch her besides Rasputin, but he was gone. She'd left him and had no intention of going back, even though she still loved him. While, in his own words, he "would be very sad if you were not near me," the most he could offer her was part-time love. Desperate to break free of the past, she met Guillaume.

Guillaume was a street musician playing hillbilly jazz. French, talented, cute. His voice was a comfort to her, since it had now been more than a month since Paris.

They went to her apartment, he admired the million dollar view. They drank beer and played *La Vie en Rose* together. They laughed. He kissed her. They went to a local pub. He kissed her again, so he either didn't mind or didn't notice she was twenty years older than him, or that she was on the spectrum. Her self-esteem had taken such a beating, half the time she imagined that there was a giant 'A' tattooed on her forehead.

She missed sex. In her life, she had gone without it for more years than people would ever believe—two and three years at a stretch without so much as a kiss from a man. She knew the consequences of its lack and the benefits of having it.

So she slept with him. The first night they were together, he couldn't perform. He had done cocaine while out with some French tourists. Artemisia was familiar with the drug. Her ex did it regularly. He had convinced her "it is what we always do" in Paris, in his circle of friends. In her naivete, it had become the new normal while she lived in France. It was also part of the reason she left. She had begun taking it herself. It was aging her, violating her body. She saw the people who did it regularly, they were years younger than her but looked much older.

She did her best to help Guillaume along, but to no avail. Still it felt so good to have someone to hold, to kiss, to sleep with, she didn't even mind. Yet, she wondered if she were cursed. Maybe she wasn't that beautiful or desirable. Maybe, like her ex had said, no one would ever love her because of the things she said. Maybe her ex was the best she would ever deserve. And he was unbelievably cruel. Had she done something terrible to deserve this?

The second time she was with Guillaume he acquitted himself admirably. He almost reminded her of Rasputin. Maybe it's a French thing—the way they approached sex was almost like fencing. An ancient art, a sport they were very good at. He brought her to orgasm without any manual or oral methods necessary. She was relieved. It was not making love, but it was fun, it was good. She was not dead yet.

But, that night Guillaume showed her a photo of a singer he'd been working with.

"People really like *her*," he said. "*She* has a really warm way about her."

She heard what he said.

"Artemisia, people do not really like *you*. You do *not* have a really warm way about you."

She felt it. She wondered why men often felt inclined to insult her by way of praising other women. Other women could not do the things that she did. Rasputin always insulted her, especially in the beginning, when they were officially a couple. Maybe this too was a cultural thing, she did not know.

She decided, as a rare snow fell on Athens, it was time for:

. . . .

RULE #2 She did not deserve insults, or cruelty.

. . . .

Her only crime in love had been to be too trusting. And, perhaps, as she would be told over and over again over the coming months, too quick to hop into bed with a man.

"I don't think we should hang out anymore," she told Guillaume politely. "It was fun and I wish all the best for you but let's leave it." She didn't think, in her entire life, that she had ever said that to anyone before. Her Aspie self usually wanted to make everything work. It was empowering to say "That was nice, thanks, and have a great life." She felt like she'd just grown up a little.

Perhaps nonautistics knew this instinctively and would say "big deal." But Artemisia was both shocked and freed by this revelation. Not everyone you slept with had to turn into a long-term boyfriend, girlfriend or spouse. You could say goodbye before the *merde* hit the fan. It was not necessarily a mistake to be intimate with someone that was not a 'forever' love. If the latter is what you want, there were ways to go about it and ways not to...she'd think about that later. For now, she had:

. . . .

RULE #3 Not every crush is true love. And that's okay.

. . . .

CHAPTER 4

LA DOLCE VITA (THE SEX DATE)

Still not fully used to the idea of being single, she found herself in the best city in the world to be single in—depending on your criteria—Rome, Italy. She was there to give a conference. Finally, she was in her element.

She sometimes preferred the more earthly delights of Rome over unearthly Athens, even over the domestic bliss she (almost) had before in Paris. And when in Roma…well, you could say she was living *la dolce vita*. There were Aspies who would hate this place. Too much 'touchy feely' sometimes, too many *buongiorno*s for some. For Artemisia, after many years of loneliness, she was loving it. She loved all the baristas, the waiters, the museum attendants, the street sellers, the musicians, the proprietors. She even loved that the number one cause of death in Rome had to be ankle failure due to the crooked cobble streets, followed by, of course, being creamed by a motorcycle whipping around a corner going in the wrong direction.

She loved the smell of espresso in the air and delicious pizza everywhere, although she could have lived without the odor of two thousand years of sewage and the sour alcohol smell in the morning after the bars closed. She loved that she had been called *Bella* more times than Artemisia. Here, she felt exotic, feminine, sweet. She was the writer and musician that handsome young men wanted to get to know—this was something quite new. She sometimes bumped into American women who didn't quite get the pace. They were ranting about politics in cafés and crying "doom!" There was a time and a place, but she'd advise them to take the time to stop and smell the cappuccino. If only she felt like talking to them. She didn't.

She met Damiano when she popped into a café to hear some jazz. Live music is a friend to the solo traveler. It gives you someone to stare at and connect with, without seeming creepy. Before she knew it, a young man poured himself a drink, sat next to her and made intelligent conversation in perfect English. She thought he was adorable in a wholesome kind of way, the way she would think about one of her daughter's friends. She left after a couple of hours and passed out early, but woke at 2AM, just moments after he messaged her.

"What are you doing?"

She'd never done anything like this before, but thought about it for a moment and replied, "Nothing, why?" After all, when in Rome...

A message. "I'm here."

She opened the door, he entered, bearing wine, pushed her up against the wall and kissed her immediately. There was no pretense. They liked each other—yes —he's smart—yes — she's more than a bimbo—yes —but this was a sex date. She had only one hesitation: she knew that, for her, the sex would not be that good. The first time with a man never was. Plus, there would have to be condoms. How she hated them.

"I hate one night stands," she told him, "so we'll have to do this again."

He said, "OK."

Damiano was, to Artemisia, the perfect first Italian—no — Roman lover. Proportionately perfect, black curls like smoke in the night, dark eyes, cupid's bow mouth, perfect skin; his only flaw would be his rather small chin. A weak chin. And also, for her, because he was proportionate and shorter than her, not perhaps as well-endowed as she'd like. He maintained a level of detachment, the way he licked, kissed, fucked, there was never a real pouring into, melting into, which she had grown used to with Rasputin and even Guillaume. Only his beauty sustained her interest, for it was considerable.

But it did not have that fire that she required, that she was used to, in sex. Not his fault, she was sure it would, next time. He slept over, and she woke with her arms cramped from holding him in a vice grip. She still missed the ex, her heart still fairly starved for affection. Damiano was genial in the morning, they did it again, despite the fact that morning sex never did it for her.

He left with a kiss, saying, "See you."

There were a few messages, she was buzzing and quite delighted for the rest of the day. Despite any shortcomings, he was attentive, gorgeous, smart and it was fun. Then after a day or two, the messages abruptly stopped. If she had known it was only for one night, she would have been fine with that, but she did clearly state they would need to do this twice. And he had said "OK."

He had told Artemisia that all women fall in love with him when he slept with them, but she honestly knew that, in her case, that would not be. Perhaps she was just lacking theory of mind, but she thought that would have been obvious and saw no reason not to send friendly messages afterward. She saw him days later in the same café, they sat together for a bit, had a relaxed and friendly conversation. Until he slipped her age into the conversation.

"I Googled you," he smiled.

She tried to be cool and said, "Don't believe everything you read on the internet."

"I have two girlfriends," he told her. "I'm exhausted... from the games and the lying. I'm overstretched."

Artemisia began to think that men were more alien to her than ever. She knew female cheaters existed, of course, but she never knew one. Women who were openly polyamorous, yes, but cheaters, no. Only men.

She felt no pity; but also, no judgment. Damiano and she parted friends.

"I'll be in touch," he said.

She never heard from him again, which in itself might have just been a time issue, as in, not enough had passed. After a couple of weeks, she messaged him, saying, "It was unnecessary to lie, you didn't have to say we'd be friends if you never intended it."

His response would not surprise anyone who did not have Aspergers: "Clearly you don't accept me for who I am. Goodbye."

Ouch. She now had:

. . . .

RULE #4 Don't scold a man after a date
because you didn't get what you wanted.

. . . .

It *never* got the results she wanted when she preached, no matter how right she was.

Maybe he *was* copping out, not ready to face the fact that maybe dishonesty isn't good. She thought of the life he was living: two women probably very much in love, and a string of lies being told on a daily basis. That would exhaust anyone. She was so glad she was no longer in that kind of relationship. She was free. But, at the end of the day, Damiano's life was none of her business.

RULE #5 A One Night Stand is just that.

She would make a note of this, not to look for a second date, or even for friendship. She didn't like the idea, but this was totally new ground for her. And…

RULE #6 If you are bringing a lover to your house, be sure to tell someone—anyone— who it is and ask them to check on you.

She did at least do that, told her closest girlfriends what she was up to, what his name was and where she met him. Not that it would have saved her life in a pinch, being that they were in Australia, NY and everywhere she was not, but it was something.

We know so little about the new people we meet, but we like who we like and love is always about taking chances— some chances being riskier than others. Still, there are no guarantees no matter how long you've known someone. How many men and women in the world live with their partner for years, only to discover later that they are a criminal or have another family?

CHAPTER 5

ONE NIGHT STANDS

Artemisia had never been a fan of the one night stand. She'd had them but almost always they were never her intention and she had tried to keep seeing the person she'd slept with. She always considered them the domain of men and shallow people. The goal of footballers, frat boys and slutty women. Were they all they were cracked up to be?

It was one of the great ironies of nature that most men are never as turned on as the first time with a new woman, but women grow into sex with a partner, so as it gets better and hotter for her, it grows more predictable and boring for him. Men—at least, this is what some have told her—could have fantastic orgasms in a one night stand, and swore that the women they 'hit and run' got as much pleasure out of it as they did. Based on her own experience, however, she doubted that.

And then, there were condoms to consider, which added—pun intended—a whole other layer to sex. Copulation is risky business and, even if you couldn't get pregnant, you could get everything else. Artemisia always had some sort of allergic reaction to condoms. So now she was faced with a Hobson's Choice. Allergy, or possibly worse? Less sensation in a situation that you already know probably won't feel as good as you'd like? And despite the odds, her periods were still regular, so technically she could be fertile yet. *Mamma mia!* How did she get here? Most women her age were tending gardens and spoiling grandkids, going on holidays with beer-bellied, grey-haired spouses they'd been with for 30 years.

And then how do you meet men? People thought it was easy for a woman to find love and a partner, especially if she was successful and/or pretty. There were so many flawed assumptions in there she barely knew where to begin. But to start with, Asperger women often possessed an intelligence and a power that could frighten, intimidate and sometimes just plain rub someone the wrong way. They could be too forthright, shocking. We've all heard about flirtatious bold Italian men? Artemisia had been the boldest thing in Trastevere since she arrived. If she liked someone, she had no problem telling them they were *"molto bello"* or that she would like an "Italian lesson." When a man was overpowered he wouldn't say so, he'd just slink away. This left her feeling like she did something wrong, but she wasn't sure what.

She was learning to be a bit more subtle. But slowly, through her mistakes.

"I am sickened by the idea of casual sex," said Elle, her grown and married daughter.

This was another thing. Everyone in the world had their own ideas about how women of a certain age, culture, background or role should behave. There are no *shoulds*.

"That is absolutely fine. You will get no judgment from me; hopefully I will get no judgment from you. What I am talking about is *authenticity*. We are chameleons, all. What we loved yesterday is not necessarily what we love today.

What we find unfathomable today might be completely acceptable tomorrow. Be authentic to where you are now. Where I am now, is a woman who enjoys sex and is sick of watching Netflix every night. Anyway, the internet connection in Europe is terrible."

She may have given up her 'happily ever after' ideals, but she had not given up on life. As she walked up the Via dei Fiori Imperiali, the Coliseum rose before her and she thought of her favorite line from the film *Gladiator, Not yet…not yet.*

RULE #7 Until you are in a mutual committed relationship and have been tested, you must use a condom.

This, like all the other rules, would be broken.

CHAPTER 6

LEONARDO

The first time Artemisia saw Leonardo was in a restaurant in Trastevere, the riverside district in Rome where she had rented a place for a month. Caffè Verona was close to her flat, played classic rock and had a bountiful *aperitivo*: mountains of couscous, cheeses, olives, peppers, salads and, of course, mouth-watering pasta. The waiters were nice—cute even—but not at all on her sexual radar. Leonardo was very young, so she spoke to him almost maternally, devoid of any flirtation. He barely knew a word of English but his retro 70s curls and sweet smile were comforting to her. His co-worker, Raffaele, was fluent, and had a thin mustache that made him look exactly like an Italian Gomez Addams. Around them, Artemisia felt right at home.

One night, after a fun but fairly frustrating outing with two men—a typical, "you're each chasing the wrong one" scenario—she stopped in to see Leonardo and Raffaele and have a nightcap. As she was about to leave, a group of inebriated young Romans piled in off the narrow street. They often traveled in packs after midnight, she noticed.

One sat next to Artemisia and slurred, "You're beautiful," and looked at Leonardo and Raffaele for assurance, as if he could not trust his drunken eyes.

They agreed. She let the young man buy her a drink, but when he drank it himself and then suddenly attached his lips to her cheek, Leonardo and Raffaele sprang into action, shouting "No" several times along with a bunch of other phrases in loud Italian that seemed to mean "get him out of here." Leo looked like he was going to leap over the bar. The young man's friends quickly grabbed him and they all left, stumbling out into the night, once more to roam the cobbled streets searching for adventure.

Artemisia was secretly delighted and ate it up like the canary-eating cat. After all, she was old enough to be their mother—all of them. Years ago, she was voted the 'worst girl in high school' and here were three hot-blooded Italian lads, fighting, in a way, over her—it was positively Shakespearean. Is it that people had changed, or had she? Or both? Was it the magic of Rome or could this happen anywhere now, even in her hometown? She had more questions than answers. But at that moment she just grinned like Mona Lisa and made the short walk home once the coast was clear.

A few nights later, after a disappointing evening in the Ego Café, where she'd met Damiano, she practically ran to the comfort of Caffe Verona on the way home, just wanting to see a familiar, friendly face. Leonardo was there, polishing the glasses, catching the light with his curls. For the first time, the gleam in his eye conveyed something sensual, clandestine. She sat at the bar and gave him an English lesson while he taught her a few words in Italian. He requested her on Facebook. She went home to find he'd already sent a message. "Give me your address." When he finished at 1AM, he came right over.

There was nothing more fabulous than having a beautiful Romeo tell you that you are *"bellissima"* while kissing your whole face. Leonardo was long, lithe, muscular, affectionate, and voracious. He pulled her hair, and grabbed her roughly. Though he kissed her and praised her beauty the whole time, like Damiano he was not as emotionally connected as she was used to. She guessed it was an Italian thing to be this way.

They didn't use condoms. Leonardo seemed so young and innocent to her and inexperienced. And, before Rasputin, her life was a vast desert of celibacy and loneliness that stretched back more years than people would believe, so she felt safe.

"Your eyes are green," said Leonardo in Italian, staring deeply into them. "Your heartbeat...it is not normal."

*He is observant—perceptive—*she thought to herself. *So he does care.*

He messaged her two days later, "Where are you? I waited for you but you didn't come. I have tomorrow off and want to see you."

She was on a date with someone else. At last, Artemisia was the pursued, not the pursuer. That in itself was something new for her, but it did spin her head around for another reason. Her new rule about one night stands was tossed on its head. She'd slept with him right away but here he was wanting to see her again. Hmmm...what's going on here?

She couldn't wait to find out; for Leonardo, she liked.

. . . .

RULE #8 There will be exceptions to the rules.

. . . .

CHAPTER 7

KNOCK FIRST

Artemisia was tired after her date with Leonardo, so the next day she decided to visit a very local museum, literally right around the corner from her flat. Across the tiny piazza, was a restaurant with a handsome *maître d* who gave her a smile as she passed. She decided to lunch there after taking in some art. Museums were something she could always count on to lift her spirits, literally to a higher place: a mini-vacation for the mind and soul.

Now for the body. At the restaurant she asked *maître d* Romero for a cigarette. He didn't smoke but he found her one. He gave her a friendly, charming smile and they chatted briefly until her pasta came—typical of these restaurants, tasty but loaded with cheese and fat and completely devoid of vegetables. Before she left, he gave her a card with his number on it. They ended up meeting later that evening at a casual 'bar'—what would be called a café in America. The place was not her style, being on a busy road and having fluorescent lights, but she was trying to rid herself of her controlling ways. He set her at ease.

Italian men had a way of making women physically and emotionally comfortable, more than other cultures, she found. They made her feel beautiful with their smiles and compliments and always with just a hint of mischief in their eyes. Their confidence was contagious rather than off-putting. These were not the macho, polyester Italians she'd seen in TV shows like the *Sopranos*. These were far more elegant creatures, stepped straight out of canvases, magazines, and marble sculptures.

A peddler appeared, trying to force some unwanted trinkets upon them. Although they politely but repeatedly said "No thank you," he showed no signs of leaving.

Artemisia pulled Romero close and said, "Kiss me," thinking that would get the vendor, and the inevitable, out of the way.

Instead of the gentle, passionate meeting of two sets of lips, she found a giant squirming live watery fish had been shoved into her mouth.

She pulled away quickly. "Oh my god!" she couldn't help but yell. "I'm sorry, but so much tongue!"

He seemed undaunted, and did it again.

"No, not like that. Like this, keep your mouth closed."

She kissed him again, the way she always kissed, but the moment she parted her lips for the gentle probing, she received her second otolaryngological exam.

Artemisia made her first:

. . . .

RULE FOR MEN ONLY, or at least, mainly.
Kiss with the lips first, tongue second. If you want
the door to open you have to knock first.

. . . .

If you kiss well with your lips, the tongue will come naturally when passions are aroused. Otherwise, it's like cutting to the head of the line…you're going to piss someone off. And maybe even get thrown to the back of the line where you've got to start all over again. Do it once more and you might get thrown out entirely.

Artemisia was an Aspie. She improved things, she made things right. "I got this." With her careful tutelage, she would make a good kisser of him. They went to another place and he bought her dinner. Their knees touched under the table the whole time, their hands often met. The food was delicious. The waitress seemed to take a keen interest in her date, which only piqued Artemisia's attraction to him. They left and went to her place.

While she never really could tame that wild wet tongue, Romero accomplished the (nearly) impossible and set off her rockets on the first night without hands, tongues or tools. *Ooh la la.* That—*not* the doorway to Tiffany's—is the way to a woman's heart.

"Where did you learn to do that?" she asked rhetorically, assuming it was part talent, part practice.

"I used to sell myself to women when I was younger, 19. I worked at a seaside resort and it just sort of happened."

Ah, well, she thought, *we have to get our money and education from somewhere. That must have been ages ago.* "How old are you now?" she asked.

"Twenty-three."

I really need to get my eyes checked, she thought, *and so did they.*

The alarm went off minutes after they fell asleep…at least that's what it seemed like. Artemisia kept waiting for Romero to drink his coffee, throw on his big boy pants and leave so she could fall back into her happy Aspie bubble.

Mornings were sacred. Mornings were made not for awkward conversations with strangers, but for enjoying the softness of cotton sheets, leaning back on pillows, catching up on Facebook, fielding emails. All the while silently enjoying her own delicious cup of sacred brew. An hour went by, and still he was there, sipping coffee and looking at his phone…in her bed! The cheek. She wanted to kill him. Seriously. She waited patiently—okay, impatiently—for signs that he was going to leave, but still he did not move. She began to worry that she was glaring at him the way her chihuahua glared at her when he wanted to be fed. Romero got a little sheepish. Finally, just when her lid was about to blow, he made to leave.

"Okay, bye."

"Okay, goodbye, thanks, that was a great night, see you around!"

She slammed the door, turned around and breathed deeply.

RULE #9 If it's a first nighter, don't let them sleep over. It's (almost) always dead awkward.

This was another rule she would break many times.

CHAPTER 8

THE PRICE OF FAME...OR AT LEAST OF GOOGLE

Leonardo had messaged when she was with Romero. "Where are you? I have the day off tomorrow. I want to see you."

He had the day off. She wanted to spend it in his arms. She was tired, not having gotten enough sleep for the last two nights, but she was eager to see him, and made that clear. They met at her place, then went to get something to drink in a restaurant, the same one she went to with Romero the night before. Unfortunately, they had same waitress, who now appeared to openly despise Artemisia. She didn't care.

She and Leonardo used a translator to talk. Despite the language barrier, she felt a connection with this lad she hadn't felt with the others. He seemed familiar.

They crossed the bridge to Isola Tiberina, the twin of Ile St. Louis in Paris. Both were tiny islands in the middle of crowded, dirty cities, with rivers flowing round them bringing fresh air and ancient history at the same time. They went to the little island's far point, close to the remnants of a medieval bridge, its glorious proportions and style still evident in the one remaining arch. She wanted to fuck outside in Rome, with Leonardo, under the gaze of a medieval bridge. Life was good.

"Artemisia, we can't. Cameras." His English was extremely limited but everyone in the world knew about surveillance at this point.

She didn't care. She grabbed him, kissed him. Undid his belt, pulled down his pants and climbed the tall lad like a monkey on a tree. Before long they could hear other people arriving. *Coitus interruptus* in the home of Latin. Fitting, since the actual original settlement of Rome was only a few hundred meters away.

They returned to her apartment, played music, laughed, kissed, had a wonderful time, although it was tedious at moments because of the language barrier. He seemed a little anxious, rushed, despite having spent the whole day with her and expressing his desire to stay the night. It was like he couldn't totally relax.

At some point in their epic date, Leonardo got out of bed and said, "I know your age. I Googled." He said it in Italian of course.

Artemisia spontaneously burst into tears. She hadn't expected those words and her own reaction surprised her. *Ouch, the price of fame—or at least, technology.*

"Is okay, I don't care." He did his best to console her in Italian and his artillery of ten English words.

They made love again. As before, he was affectionate, kissed her, comforted her. She was convinced.

He got them some pizza. When he returned, he smoked some weed, and put on some strange, melancholy music. The air became thick, heavy. Then, after this epic date of ten hours, Leonardo's girlfriend joined them.

"I miss my girlfriend," he suddenly said.

"What?" Artemisia laughed. "You don't have a girlfriend."

"*Si*, I told you."

While he'd mentioned it the first time they'd met, she hadn't believed him, mainly because she never saw the girl so, therefore, she didn't really exist. But there was another reason.

"Leonardo, your Facebook page says 'single.'"

"*Scusami*, Artemisia," he said and left, fairly quickly despite her protests.

She was hurt, crushed even. It was a violent ending to an absolutely lovely day. Was it the wine they drank? She supposed she could blame a bit on that. The weed he smoked? That probably had something to do with it. She laid in her bed, unexpectedly alone, fighting back tears of regret and the urge to say, "Life's not fair!"

Or was it? There were so many 'rules'—common sense things that her own non-Aspie daughter knew when she was 14—broken on that day that she could barely list them all. But through her wine-and-shock-induced tears, she tried:

. . . .

RULE #10 Be patient. Wait to sleep with someone and don't seem too eager.

. . . .

That is, if you want more than a one night stand. But sometimes it's so hard to know…until it's too late. She liked him. If she really wanted to see him again, she should not have slept with him so quickly. But he was so young, how could she know they would have such a good time together? She was impatient. She'd asked her daughter, when Elle was about 20, what the secret to her dating success was.

"I withhold sex," Elle said.

To which Artemisia replied, "Exactly who are you punishing?" Because in her book, she'd be the one to suffer. Sigh.

. . . .

RULE #5 *again*. You cannot build a
relationship with a one night stand.

. . . .

She'd heard it a million times, she just never believed it. Part of her still didn't want to. As with all rules, she wanted to be the exception.

. . . .

RULE #11 If they say they have a girlfriend, believe
them. (If they say they *don't*, don't immediately believe *that*.)

. . . .

Don't downplay it in your mind. If it was nothing, they would have said nothing. Reading between the lines is difficult for an Aspie but, in this case, she didn't even have to. He told her and it still didn't register...because she didn't want it to.

. . . .

RULE #12 If he looks like a boy, then he
probably is. Ask your trusted friends!

. . . .

She showed her Aspergirls his picture and their reaction was "major cutey" but also, "Artemisia, he's a child!" While not literally, in every meaningful sense of the word, he was. She liked younger men for sex and dating. But there was no way it could have a future. Thirty years difference was almost always too much. But yet, men do it all the time...

CHAPTER 9

DOUBLE STANDARDS

Artemisia was sick and tired of the world having double standards. Actor Bruce Willis married someone 27 years his junior around the same time his ex-wife Demi married a man 16 years younger than her. Demi's new marriage—triumph or scandal, depending on who you asked—was all anyone talked about. The last few men Artemisia dated were decades younger than her. Sometimes, as in Leo's case, three.

She had always been a bit 'age blind,' or at least age-uncaring, finding some older men extremely attractive when she was young. Truth is, she genuinely liked people of all ages. For dating and sex, she simply preferred younger men. For true love…well, she wasn't sure if she believed in it anymore.

People often said that she was like a kid sometimes. That was the delightful and dangerous thing about people with Aspergers. They could be 100 intellectually, but emotionally be forever stuck on up the seesaw at age 12. Besides looking younger than their age, sometimes considerably, they in turn had a kind of age blindness that ran alongside face blindness. Artemisia could clearly tell the difference between a child and a 22-year-old man, but maybe some couldn't. Of course, this could allow some to sail into dangerous waters.

Leonardo, like the others, did not have a clue about *her* age…until he Googled her. She didn't know that information was public until Damiano. That would now separate the men from the boys. There were plenty of couples out there—and she knew a few—where the woman was significantly older than her partner. Sometimes it can and does work. But Leonardo was not on the spectrum. He was a social, non-Aspie male who didn't speak the same language as her. It was highly unlikely anything could have developed. Could it?

At least she had done the impossible, she had begun dating. And, despite the knocks, she was enjoying it. There was life after Rasputin, after heartbreak. She was learning so much she decided to write a book about it. She began to think of herself as the Aspie version of Carrie Bradshaw, minus the expensive shoes. It was her job to date, in the name of research.

She had discovered that while, yes, people could be scary for those on the autism spectrum, they all ultimately wanted the same thing—to be loved, liked and appreciated. She now knew some things that seemed impossibly mysterious when she was younger; for example, sometimes all you needed to break the ice were a smile and a friendly *hello*. It wasn't rocket science but, for Aspies, rocket science was easy. This stuff? Much harder.

She still made mistakes. She raised an eyebrow for every head that she turned. She had always had an unwavering belief in herself. But belief was not the same thing as love. She was beginning to realize:

. . . .

RULE #13 You have to love yourself, have a strong
healthy relationship with yourself, before you can
be comfortable being with someone else. This one
would be tested more than some of the others.

. . . .

In Rome, for the first time in her life, every day she heard that
she was beautiful. Was it disingenuous? Not necessarily. Was
it true love? Not likely. The two were not mutually exclusive.
She learned, or at least was learning:

. . . .

RULE #14 When a man wants to sleep with a
woman he may be the kind that will say *anything*.

. . . .

He will be very nice, or at least present himself in a way that
he deems sexy. And again, like all these rules, she would from
time to time, forget. Which is why she needed:

. . . .

RULE #15 Learn to laugh at your
own mistakes. Not at yourself.

. . . .

She would have to, or she would retreat, go crazy, give up.
And what then?

The fictional Carrie was surrounded by neurotypical
girlfriends. Artemisia was digitally surrounded by *Aspergirls*.
Not quite the same thing as being in the same space as
someone, but still invaluable. She was the President of the
Club that she had founded. They were an ever-growing legion

of Asperger sisters, not subjects. They gave Artemisia advice, a sounding board and protection, while she forged ahead to see what she could learn about life and this thing called love.

When she'd left Rasputin, it was these women she turned to. When Leonardo aborted himself abruptly from her bed, it was that these women she wrote to. Each time she felt her courage fail, her will falter, she'd write or Skype with one of them. She had always wanted many girlfriends but, in the land of neurotypicals, she had never had a tribe. She now did.

. . . .

RULE #16 It is absolutely necessary to have female friends you can trust to get their advice.

. . . .

No one is infallible, we all make bad choices, and if seven of your girlfriends are saying the same thing but opposing you, who do you think is likely right?

CHAPTER 10

ARRIVEDERCI ROMA

Two days later Artemisia went to see Leonardo and Raffaele at Verona. She ordered a big meal instead of her usual *aperitivo*. She wanted to let him know that there were no hard feelings, but also that she was a woman of independent means who could take herself out to dinner, while he was merely the one who would have to wait on her. It turned out that Raffaele was the one to spring to her table. She did not talk to Leonardo but she winked at him, and she caught him smiling fondly at her once or twice. She spoke with Raffaele a bit, and then she left. She did not return to Verona on that trip.

Two days later, before she caught her plane back to Athens, she woke to a message: "Where are you? I waited for you last night. I wanted to say goodbye."

She was so startled she jumped out of bed, forgetting she fell asleep with headphones on. They were still attached to her tablet, which went flying and knocked over everything that was on her bedside table. Her first trip to Rome ended with spilled wine and broken glass. She didn't care, she didn't see the omen, she was simply happy. In some strange way, Artemisia loved Leonardo.

She did not message back. She wanted to leave it on a high note.

. . . .

RULE #17 You must leave someone you care about, if you know there's no way it can be healthy or happy for either of you, before it gets ugly.

. . . .

CHAPTER 11

IT'S ALL GREEK TO HER

Back in Athens, she was frustrated, lonely, despite having more friends—or at least acquaintances—there. Greek men just didn't have the same forward sexuality as Romans. A helpful bartender told her that Greek men were more subtle—that they liked to know the person had a bit more going on, even if it was a one night stand. That was all well and good, but she missed the Italians who laid it all on the table like an *aperitivo*, saying, "It's yours if you want it."

Maybe it was just as well she had to take time to regroup and restock. The Roman way had caused her to rush into things. As an Aspie, she heard what was being said, so she liked it to be good. She sensed the person underneath it all, so that had to be good too, or she sensed danger. What she missed was the operative level, the one in the middle. The one that made even a nice man say nice things but do shitty things. That was the level most at play in the world of sexual conquest and that was the one hardest for her to discern.

When you have Aspergers, you may have a great faculty for language but, when you try to express how you feel, subtlety is lost. If you like someone, you say, "I like you"; when you love someone, you say, "I love you." You might even say to someone you have not yet been intimate with, "I'd like to have sex with you." When you miss someone, you say, "I miss you." That is, *if* you know how you feel. That took time—decades, perhaps. This directness could be shocking because it could also show up as, "I don't like you" or "I don't find you attractive." Even, in the case of some relationship gone bad, "I hope you get hit by a truck."

If she tried to be coy or subtle, like a neurotypical woman, invariably she cocked it up. She did get good at sarcasm though. From time to time when she was bored, she'd send Rasputin a greeting card, saying things like: *You may wear Italian suits and Rolex watches but your taste in women is strictly Walmart.* Childish, yes, but it helped pass the time, and it also happened to be true. Like many Aspies, he was unable to tell the proverbial silk purse from the sow's ear and would have whoever wanted him. Literally.

In Athens, where people were perhaps not so direct, she might have been seen as a kind of simpleton. She didn't care, really. After a lifetime of being suppressed and overwhelmed to the point of mutism, there was no shutting her up now. There was great joy in self-expression, whether it was a happy giggle or the occasional cutting remark.

She'd lived in Rome, Athens and Paris for over a year now and didn't speak any of those languages fluently. It bothered her a little. It reminded her of being a teenage Aspie again, sitting with a group of alleged peers, not understanding a thing anyone was saying or being able to predict where the conversation might go. She'd end up frozen and mute much of the time, then go home and watch Monty Python which she understood perfectly, or read the encyclopedia. Once she stopped crying, that is. These days she just sipped her wine and enjoyed the thoughts in her own head, or tried to guess what everyone was saying, if she felt ambitious.

She went to sleep at night watching foreign films, hoping her subconscious would perform some magic tricks in the night and she'd wake up fluent. She never did. But she was learning how to just be happy and relaxed, and rely less on language. It was better now that she knew that people everywhere wanted the same thing—to be liked, understood and appreciated. You could communicate so much with minimal words. Some of her new friends spoke no English, and they felt real affection for each other although at times there were impasses. You might use sign language and play like little children one moment, and then hit a wall trying to communicate more sophisticated concepts. That made her sad at times, knowing that you could get a feeling for a person but never really know their innermost thoughts. Perhaps that was part of the problem with Rasputin. He knew her language but she didn't know his. He was a bad, impatient teacher, criticizing her even when when she was right, wasting time on arguments only to admit three minutes later she had said something correctly. It felt like sabotage, like he didn't want her to be fluent. That way he had something over on her and could communicate in secret even when she was near. Like the time he made a date with his ex-girlfriend right in front of her.

"I can come too," Artemisia had said.

Language problems had their surreal moments, like when one of her friends had to cancel on her because, he said, "I am with a *big chick*." Actually, she found out later, he'd had had his wisdom tooth pulled and had a *"swollen cheek."*

Perhaps it would be wiser to study the nonverbal communication of autistics and animals more, in order to exercise our own telepathic, nonverbal communication, rather than trying to make autistics communicate verbally. We all read thoughts from time to time.

As many Aspies had told her, "I have good instincts, I just don't listen to them."

. . . .

RULE #18 Even a nice person who says nice things can do shitty ones in the game of sexual conquest.

. . . .

. . . .

RULE #19 Learn to listen to and trust your instincts. Words are not the only form of communication.

. . . .

Silence is full of information.

CHAPTER 12

SCANDAL AND WISDOM

When you were 24, and an Aspergirl, you wanted people to notice you for your mind, your character and your talents. When you were Artemisia's age, you may want to be noticed for your looks—let's face it—tits, lips and ass. What's wrong with that? Nature created women to be provocative to males to induce the procreation of the species. The sexier you were, the more likely you were to get impregnated. She was not interested in the latter, but the process was still quite appealing to her. She didn't want a house in the burbs with a man who came home from work, went on his laptop, read the paper or, worse, flirted on some dating app. She wanted to go dancing. She wanted to be courted, taken out to dinner, taught Italian by a naked man.

However, she didn't always look sexy for that reason. Sometimes she just dressed for whimsy. One Sunday she put on the most scandalous outfit she owned—a tight, red top with a plunging neckline, a miniskirt that was more of a wide belt, stay-up stockings, black boots and over-the-knee socks. She covered it all with a modest pink raincoat. She wore it for her. It was a fun outfit, the kind of thing a Japanese *Harajuku* might wear on her day off.

In Plaka, one man's jaw dropped so far Artemisia actually had to ask him, "Are you alright?" as she thought he was having some kind of seizure. He didn't answer but kept staring wide-eyed long after closing his mouth.

She decided to leave the crowds, avoid people and walk on the nature paths of Acropolis among the trees and ancient ruins, the wind, the hazy clouds, the myriad cats. When she encountered gawkers, she merely smiled; if they were bold, she laughed. Not *at* them, but to let them know they had nothing to be jealous or insecure about. Most human nastiness seemed to be born of those things...and greed.

Stepping off the paths and back onto a road, she ran into the one person she didn't want to see...a notoriously jealous wife of a friend who, disingenuously, said, "You look nice."

Artemisia cut right to the chase and responded, "I look like a prostitute, but I'm comfortable and happy."

Then the conversation moved on to other things—to the cats that this woman helped care for. There were thousands of strays in the city, lounging under every bush and tree, and she helped feed, medicate and castrate them. A necessary thing, unfortunately, or the streets would literally be paved with cat.

On the walk home, Artemisia began to fully realize that young women in high school, offices, the conservative world, could not be so free. They could acquire that nasty little thing called a reputation which caused a girl to lunch alone, to receive looks, gestures and comments that she didn't even understand, much less want to accept. Younger Aspergirls particularly needed to hear that. Even as a mature, self-employed woman, Artemisia had been professionally impacted negatively by gossip. No one was completely immune, but while Artemisia could get a reputation among some, certainly, she was not particularly bothered. She was not trapped inside four walls but had the luxury of being able to walk away. She had that delicious little thing called Freedom and no one to answer to but her own conscience.

She was an artist, and daily kissed that hallowed path of self-expression. As she sauntered home, she also mentally kissed the ground she walked on, because it seemed here in Athens, close to Parthenon, the wisdom of the ages was literally falling down off the mountain and straight into her head.

RULE #20 Life can be made or ruined by gossip and reputation.

Men gossip too, just like women. Only they call it "talking with their friends about stuff."

RULE #21 Most human nastiness seemed to be born of jealousy, insecurity, and greed. Once you realize that, it's easier to control your own reactions.

CHAPTER 13

GETTING STOOD UP

It was a beautiful Sunday in Athens. The streets were full of people, too many for her liking, but she was happy because she had a date with Caligulis. He had suggested a visit to Parthenon together and she was looking forward to it. He seemed knowledgeable about Greek history and was a bit alternative like her, with tattoos and an outside-of-the-box view of things.

They had a date the other night. He was someone that had been on her radar for a while, because he was that rarest of things—an Athenian that had asked her out. She'd always said no, thinking he was beneath her, a bit too street. But when they bumped into each other on the street, on her first day back, she thought *Why not?* The next thing she knew she was looking at a 2000 year old temple, drinking a beer and being passionately kissed by a handsome half-Greek, half-Egyptian man with mysterious eyes.

They parted for a few hours and then met on her balcony for drinks—wine, Acropolis, starlight, of course they slept together. It was good. She was getting more adept at the one night stand and, as far as she was concerned, once with Caligulis was enough. He, however, wanted to take it further. He asked her out.

"It's free museum day Sunday. Let's go to Parthenon."

"Are you sure?" This was a clear violation of protocol.

"Absolutely," he replied.

She thought about it for a moment. It was free museum day, they were both going to go, so they might as well go together. Not exactly a date then. But yet...

She kept herself busy that morning, put on a pretty dress, bought locally-made sandals to wear on the pebble paths that led to the top of formidable Acropolis. She picked out something to leave as an offering for Athena. She waited for a message from Caligulis. It didn't come. She called, he didn't answer. She finally went, alone. Treading the steep path leading up to the Temples, every step became heavier and harder. Maybe it was the too-bright sun, maybe it was being surrounded by affectionate couples, but she just couldn't finish the climb alone. She wanted answers. She thought about everything she had learned about man/woman relationships and knew it would be better if she just didn't call. But of course, Artemisia simply could not compute being stood up.

As the white pebbles ground under her heavy steps, so too did thoughts grind under the weight of indignation: When a man hurts you, do you take it quietly, or do you speak your mind? Do you ignore him? Pretend you're not bothered? If pretending you weren't bothered (as women had been doing for centuries) worked, men wouldn't get such pleasure out of bedding women and disappearing, scot-free.

She didn't ask for a second date. She would have been perfectly happy without one. He insisted, and then proceeded to stiff her. And they say women are bitches? If a woman defends herself, she just looks like a jilted lover. If she doesn't, he gets away with it. It's a lose/lose situation.

So with nothing more to lose, she called. Finally, he answered, sounding sheepish.

"You owe me the courtesy of an explanation."

"I just checked my phone," he said. "I have an emergency situation," he said, "with my little sister."

Oh brother. He might as well have said, "My head fell off," for all she believed him.

But what she said was, "You ruined my day."

Truth is, he did. It was outside of her comprehension to let another person down. Unless there was a fire, and his phone was in the midst of the conflagration, there was simply no reason not to call. A neurotypical girl might say "what an asshole" and meet some girlfriends and have a good laugh about it. An Aspergirl goes home and writes and tries to figure out human nature and why it was so fucked. It may take the rest of her life to attempt this, and she may never succeed. But one thing she did know for sure, is that it was rude, inconsiderate.

Aspies tend to blame ourselves for others' behavior and retreat to our video games and episodes of whatever TV series we are currently obsessed with. Instead, she decided to put this experience into a bubble, and release it. She would put her happy face back on and go back out into the world, knowing full well more of these scrapes were in front of her. She would live life to the fullest. If other people were afraid of it, or of her, that was their problem.

She sent him a message: "If I'd known you were just a ho, I'd have happily paid you the 25 quid you were worth and sent you on your way." It cheered her up, if only for a moment.

Still, the next day she was distraught and felt the tendrils of depression coming up from the earth and grabbing her limbs, trying to pull her down. The sexually-free lifestyle could send an emotionally fragile person into a tailspin. She was still not sexually-savvy, nor capable of making long-term healthy choices. She needed someone to talk to, someone kind.

She went to see Tinman. He worked across the narrow pedestrian road from Caligulis and had been observing his efforts to trap Artemisia all winter long.

"I was afraid that would happen," said Tinman. "Do not be a victim. You are a grown woman. Act like it."

It shocked her to be scolded so blatantly by her friend, but she knew immediately he was right. She thanked him, mentally put on her big girl pants, texted a friend and got on with her life.

Weeks later, she got a message from Caligulis, as if nothing was wrong. "Where are you? I'm back from Swiss."

From *Swiss*. Dumbass. And it was clear this was something he was copying and pasting to probably everyone he knew. She hit 'delete' and kept talking with her friends.

. . . .

RULE #22 If someone cannot make their date with you, as long as they are not incapacitated, there is no excuse for not calling or telling you in advance. Anything less is unacceptable.

. . . .

. . . .

RULE #23 You are a grownup. If someone behaves badly, act like one, even if they don't.

. . . .

CHAPTER 14

ROMEOS AND VAMPIRES

Filos was working for her cellphone provider. They had chatted. He had a familiar, easy way about him.

"Can I message you, call you sometime?"

He already had her phone in his hand and all her details, so she replied, "Why not?"

After receiving Tinman's words of wisdom, Artemisia texted her new friend.

"What are you doing?"

"Let me take you for a bite to eat," he suggested.

After a chocolate cocktail and some doughy forgettable food, they walked along the cobbled street near the ancient Agora.

Filos pointed at a precipice of Acropolis and said, "A long time ago a young couple threw themselves off that cliff for love—their parents would not let them be together. Just like Romeo and Juliet."

"That was not a love story. Romeo was an obsessive," she replied. "Romeo was pining for Rosaline, and then immediately forgot her when he saw Juliet. He was born to pine. He had to have an obsession or he could not live."

A lot of Aspies were like that, including Artemisia herself. She knew it. As they walked she thought that maybe she constantly set herself up for failure so that she would always long for someone.

If she accepted this, would it stop?

Many of her favorite female artists over the years, Janis Joplin, Amy Winehouse, Judy Garland, Billie Holiday, directly or indirectly killed themselves over a man or, more accurately, the lack of one. They were a cautionary tale. They were women born to pine—one just had to listen to them sing. The men they obsessed over may have been one in a million, but that still meant there were thousands more like them. On some level these women chose to believe *he* (the one that left or the one that hadn't arrived yet) was the only one worthy of her love, time, energy and soul. Hence, she chose to die.

"I'm a big believer in soulmates but I believe, like puzzle pieces, we are closely tied to more than one person in our lives. Lose one, we will meet another, eventually. I'm sure of it."

Across from Parthenon was Muse Hill. The monument at its summit looked so much like Dracula's castle in the Francis Ford Coppola movie (at least from a distance), that Artemisia was sure it was the inspiration for it. She was surrounded by myths; her head was filled with them: Greek gods, popstars, Romeo and vampires. Obsession lies at the heart of so many myths. It is the *real* vampire...even killing Dracula himself when he obsessed over Mina.

Filos seemed to enjoy her philosophies and didn't seemed threatened by her intellect. Many men were, becoming angry at her choice of words.

"No one will ever love you because of the things you say," Rasputin had said.

"Why do you have to use such fancy words?" asked a husband. She had said "nauseous." He wanted her to only say "sick." What was it about some men that they needed a woman dumber than them?

Yet she had obsessed over both of them. If she had the chance to re-do life, she would have kicked them both out of her atmosphere faster than invading cockroaches in her kitchen.

RULE #24 Obsession is the real vampire. A time waster, a depleter of talent, self-love, money, everything.

It is not love, she decided. If she caught herself doing it again, she would find something (or someone) else to do.

CHAPTER 15

BRIDGES AND HOPE

Artemisia had always believed in True Love, but now she wasn't sure. After all, live long enough and it was almost guaranteed that you would tire of your companion and require fresh input, fresh blood. So, was it healthier to abandon the search for Mr. Right, in favor of Mr. Right Now?

Before Rasputin, a lover said that she'd always be a "transitional girl," meaning someone that you see between *real* girlfriends. She had the wisdom and wherewithal to listen to those whom fate put in her path. So she asked herself the question—could it be true? Was she just a bridge, and if so, could she make peace with that? After all, where would the world be without bridges?

Nevertheless, it hurt...deeply. She had less hope, even if she wasn't completely hopeless. So... What did hope become when it was downgraded? Pragmatism. Find a lover, find a friend, find something to do. Life was a series of grabbing for ropes, looking for a life preserver...looking for a bridge. No one was immune, not her, not anyone.

Too often people confused idealism with hope. Idealists fell hardest. Having a Disney view of love got so many into trouble. But what if she got lucky and met the Prince with the right shoe? What then? What happened after the ride into the sunset?

A soulmate can become a cellmate faster than you can say, "It's your turn to do the dishes."

It was a tightrope she trod, between heart and mind, body and soul, true love and using her time wisely. She still could not decide if A) she believed in true love and if she did B) whether she believed in it for herself.

. . . .

RULE #25 Don't lose hope.
Downgrade it to pragmatism.

. . . .

CHAPTER 16

CREEPERS

. . . .

RULE #26 There are few women-haters in the world
that know they are women-haters. They just like to use
the word 'bitch' a lot and other 'intelligent' phrases.

. . . .

They think a woman is great, as long as she displays no
autonomy or critical thought. The moment she does, she is a
'man-hater with penis envy.'

Here in Plaka, this touristy area where she lived, Artemisia
made friends with the buskers, butchers, baristas and the
wranglers like Tinman and Caligulis, whose job it was to lure
customers in. This creepy wrangler seemingly just came out
of nowhere one day and started shouting her name (wrongly)
across the square every time he'd spy her with his beady little
eye. He was a friend of Caligulis and gave her a bad feeling
right away, even before their date. Then, one day, as she
walked past, he grabbed her arm.

NO! Unacceptable...even from people she knew a hundred times better.

"Don't touch me!" she shouted, wrenching her arm away. She walked quickly on.

It wasn't a cultural thing. No one else there had ever done that. There was just a feeling of creepy familiarity from this person that really made her skin crawl. He kept talking to her every single time she walked by. When she spoke with Tinman, who worked ten feet away, he walked near and eavesdropped. It was painfully obvious. She didn't even know his name, she simply referred to him as 'Creeper.'

Tonight she tilted her umbrella as she walked past, so she didn't have to look at his ugly mug. He stuck his head under its periphery to grin at her. It was not a nice grin. The whole thing reeked of confrontation. So she let him have it. She wasn't shrill but she wasn't a fragile flower either. "I'm sick of you harassing me every time I walk past."

"What are you talking about?"

"You grabbed my arm as I walked by."

He got that stupid look in his eye that stupid people get when they're being stupid and said, "You're a liar."

"I want to speak to your boss," she demanded.

"He's not here."

"Of course he isn't. Apologize for calling me a liar!"

"Fuck off!"

She stood her ground. Tinman's evening replacement, a short but tough-looking girl, seemed about ready to take Creeper's side and get physical if needed.

"You better leave or I'll call the cops," he sneered.

Artemisia called his bluff. "Go ahead."

Of course he didn't. She wasn't afraid of him and she wasn't going to let him bully her. She looked around and saw other workers from a nearby café standing around pretending not to watch. No one came to her aid. The ones from the square that she knew, that liked her, they were a bit farther away and out of earshot. Or so she told herself.

When you were an Aspergirl alone, stuff like this could happen. But having a man with you was no guarantee that it wouldn't either. Some men didn't like to make waves so, in the past when things like this started to go down, her partners either ignored it, or worse, tried to make nice with the man. It was always a fatal blow to her affection for them.

"You're too confrontational," her friend Stavros would say later, even though he also added, "Everyone hates that guy, he's an asshole."

"You haven't had to put up with this shite for years and years," she responded. Men had no idea.

She passed Creeper in the street one last time on that trip. He was more aggressive than ever, and as she calmly strolled past, he shouted a Greek insult at her. She was sure it meant 'bitch.'

Months later, her third time back, she visited Tinman at his work post outside a little restaurant. He was always there—rain, snow, or shine. He felt stuck in his job, like a lot of men in Greece. That was why she called him 'Tinman,' after the woodsman who got stuck in one place after working through a downpour. That, and his very kind heart.

"Where's Creeper?"

"He is gone. He opened a restaurant...on an island."

"What island?" She wanted to be sure to avoid that one.

"Don't know." He smiled.

She got the feeling 'went to an island' was code for 'got fired and is hiding in his parents' house playing video games.' At least, she hoped so. She wasn't sure if she believed in karma anymore, but this was a good case for it. Or maybe

Athena couldn't stand having such a turd of a man in her close vicinity. Either way, Artemisia won.

. . . .

RULE #27 Bad men abound, but
good ones are out there too.

. . . .

The trick was to find one that was single and to recognize his worth when you did find him.

. . . .

RULE #28 Karma's a bitch…if you are.

. . . .

CHAPTER 17

THE QUICKIE

Like most Aspergirls, Artemisia preferred partners who were soulful, intelligent, sensitive. If a man looked at her like a piece of meat, he was totally repugnant to her. She'd never give herself away to someone who didn't have some sort of depth, who wasn't 'Aspie-friendly,' if not Aspie himself.

But if a man was a skilled actor, he might fool her for just a little while. Nikis was a charmer who got her to agree to meet him for a date. She didn't know him well and didn't trust him yet, beyond a baseline of neutral. So they met during the day for a drink. He took her to the noisiest outdoor restaurant in the whole city, and chose a table next to a very loud, very drunk group of older friends that looked like they were celebrating a reunion, or wedding, or something. They were jolly and singing old Greek songs, the embarrassing kind. Artemisia was happy for them, that they had such cause and capacity for merriment, but it was just too loud for her, and she told Nikis so. This was something she didn't do too often anymore, having achieved a level of adeptness in managing her sensory issues. But, to be fair, Greek volume dials go up to 11.

"I don't want to move. I need the sun," he said stubbornly.

She pointed to another table that was partly bathed in light and he agreed to move. This was not off to the best start. He ordered two beers, no food. She didn't recall him asking if she was hungry. Again, not the best first impression.

"I'm a simple guy, what you see is it," he stated with a fairly uninteresting blank look.

Artemisia, being the Sherlock Holmes of the psyche, or so she fancied, couldn't just get up and leave, she had to analyze and investigate. She thought, *No, there must be more than this.* So, she decided to be nice to him, kind, disarm him.

"I'm writing a book about sex," she told him, knowing that he wouldn't be able to resist.

"Maybe you can help me with my problem," he said, sincerely. "I can't last in sex very long."

She wasn't about to play counselor with her date, but she gave him a few choice words of advice.

"Maybe you need to try and connect with each woman, instead of attacking her as if she were a thing."

His phone rang, or he pretended it did. He had to go to work. Thank god. She didn't care if he was lying, she was relieved. They parted amicably, an expression in his blue eyes something she couldn't discern, her reflection in their shallow depths not someone she recognized.

She resolved not to see this unevolved man again. It had taken a very long time for her to realize that there were different levels of intelligence, maturity, sophistication, and depth. But also, Consciousness.

. . . .

RULE #29 If you feel someone is 'not on your level' they probably aren't, and you can feel okay about that. It doesn't make you a snob.

. . . .

She happened to bump into Nikis again a week or so later. He called her name, she turned around. He was beaming and clearly glad to see her.

They hugged. "How you doing?" she asked with real curiosity, he seemed so different.

"Lots of girls, lots of dates." Then he added, "My whole approach is different...thanks to you."

"To me?" She thought she might have made some impression but not to this extent.

"I am taking my time, talking with them, getting to know them, feeling affectionate."

At least it was a step in the right direction for him.

A week later, he texted her. Curiosity compelled her to see what she had done. She had her first real booty call, meaning she went into it knowing it was just that and could never be anything more.

It was sex, on a table, not great, but not bad. And actually, what was unfathomable to her weeks ago, was fun. In fact it was the least harmful of all her recent encounters because she didn't want him, beyond the moment, for anything.

He lasted, he said, "longer than usual."

She said goodbye to him immediately after. Artemisia: sex therapist? She was not sure they were supposed to be quite this hands-on.

He texted her again a few days later. "Want to have coffee?"

"No thanks," she wrote back and continued her walk through the teeming market of Monastiraki, knowing he was just meters away. Ah, freedom. It is a good thing.

. . . .

RULE #30 Booty calls can be healthy, if you practice safe sex and have no expectations beyond what it is. But, they are not for everyone!

. . . .

Some women are capable of sound choices, others aren't and need a trusted friend or counselor to guide them. Some women on the spectrum even choose celibacy because they can't trust their own judgment. You might feel violated, used, it might go against your deepest most dearly held inclinations. Your morality is personal to you, and shouldn't be violated. Expanded, perhaps, if and when you are ready, but if someone goes too far against their own character just for the sake of it, they might do some damage to themselves.

It was not for Artemisia to live for the whole world, only for herself. She was the night watchmen, on the tower, first to face danger. And she was loving it.

CHAPTER 18

HAPPINESS

There are people in the world who spend their whole life chasing happiness from without. They buy boats, cars, planes, trains, corporations, islands, trying to amass as much stuff as they can to see where happiness lies. Maybe they have a great time, but if wealth (and fame) were everything, so many rich people wouldn't overdose in hotel rooms across the globe, enter rehab, psychotherapy.

Sometimes people spend all their time and money searching for happiness and when they don't find it, they do a 180 and turn to a higher power—do good works, pray, lunch with lamas on a mountaintop in Tibet, looking for the meaning of it all.

Then there are those who innately feel that happiness comes from within—these are usually folk from humbler origins who never had the chance to see where else it might lie. They bake bread, grow flowers, look for joy in the simple things. They do yoga, have friends with names like Mantra and Saffron.

Artemisia firmly believed happiness was found in a combination of all of the above.

One of her female scientist friends told her, "When a particle finds itself alone, isolated, it will gravitate toward the most similar particle it can find. I'm putting it simply, but this is the gist of it."

"Ah, so when you go through your day, if you are a pillar of misery and pain, you will attract more misery and pain. If you go through the day full of joy and optimism, you're more likely to attract that which brings you more joy and optimism?"

"Basically yes."

There is a little more than the law of attraction. There's always destiny to consider, if you believe in it. Fate. And sometimes, shit just seems to happen.

When she was six years old she prayed like a good little Christian that god would make her life very hard so that she would have a chance to prove her character and worth. She needn't have bothered. When you have Aspergers you have a long life ahead of you filled with adversity, and tough times were already there. But she had the thing that she valued and sometimes hated the most about Aspergers: Constant striving for perfection, fortitude, the inability to give up until you have made something right. That is why we stay in bad situations for too long. Trying to make something right that cannot be made right. But, on the other hand, it is the same quality that shines from within, the quality that makes people stand up and take notice, that confuses them about our age, and why we are a little different.

Caligulis had stared at her eyes for a long time wondering aloud what color they were.

"Green encircled by brown," she had told him. What she should have said was "autistic." While he'd pronounced them "strange but sexy" she knew what he didn't. Those eyes looked at the world as if from outer space sometimes, wondering how the hell she got here and where she would go when she left.

Sometimes, she wished people knew what she'd been through and would part like the Red Sea when she walked by. But, if she were going to be honest with herself, that was just seeking pity, and it just might attract more things that created the *need* for pity.

. . . .

RULE #31 Let people think you've led a charmed life. Maybe they will attract it for you.

. . . .

CHAPTER 19

BEING LONELY

"Are you alone?" asked the Greek waitress in a loud voice. She sounded like she was gloating—maybe over her mastery of the question in English, maybe over the fact that she didn't like Artemisia's face and was glad no one else did either.

Artemisia was feeling too sensitive today.

In some languages "I'm alone" is the same as "I'm lonely." She was beginning to tire of the idea of being single. Not that she ever really embraced it. She never wanted to be out there again. Having many first dates was like reading the first chapter from several different books, rather than reading one whole one. She began to crave a good book. But how to find one? The advice given to women was contradictory.

Sethos, the handsome waiter from her first trip (they'd become *almost* friends), said to her, "Sex first, then love comes after."

But he was trying to set her up with his buddy so he couldn't be trusted, even if he was an otherwise decent bloke.

"I don't believe you," she replied. He just grinned and walked away.

Men can be cute, adorable, largely kind, but these same men can use you in a heartbeat and have no concern for your emotional wellbeing afterward. It's very hard for an Aspergirl to get her brain around this.

How do you meet someone? Her last two relationships were an old crush who found her online, and another Aspie who knew her work and reputation and sought her out for rather sinister and selfish reasons—to advance his career and make another woman jealous.

Many people meet their partners on dating sites; in fact, several of her Aspergirl friends had. One met her new love through a friend's Facebook post about a man who heroically saved a wounded crow. She wrote to him and next thing you know, true love bells were ringing through the Canadian Rockies. Another met her husband at an AS support group she ran. Others through work, through friends, simply walking down the street. Artemisia? Not so lucky.

Sometimes she thought she was too fussy, but then she looked back at the liaisons she'd had and thought "maybe I'm not fussy enough." Fuzzy, more like. She had one or two nice guys that were interested in her now, but she just didn't feel like there was enough common ground there. She was attracted to beautiful bad boys. Even when they disguised themselves as good men and she thought, *Right, here's a keeper*, he just turned out to be Voldemort in Batman's clothing.

In Rome, she started smoking again just a little, because A) she was nervous and upset that her bathroom kept flooding, and B) it was one way to meet men.

She'd walk up to one in the square and say "Do you have a cigarette? I don't really smoke enough to buy them."

Of course she didn't ask just anyone, she'd find men who looked like they just got out of work and were enjoying a glass of wine in the piazza. Or, who were working in a restaurant. It worked well enough to get her invited to sit and join them for a drink. Sometimes it got her a dinner date. But none of them turned out to be true love, because it was just too random. And, ironically, the last thing she wanted was a relationship with another smoker!

In Athens, it was much harder. They were much more reserved than Italians, so even if they gave you a cigarette, they didn't usually ask you out afterward. Some simply stared at you like meerkats as you walked past. When you were Artemisia, saver of countless Aspie marriages, you were supposed to be living in a tower with Prince Charming (why was he never a 'King,' anyway?) feeding you grapes, protecting you from harm and making mad passionate love to you every night in a four poster with stars for your ceiling.

How the hell would she meet someone? She wanted to meet Colin Farrell. How did one do that? She wanted to be Halle Berry and have a gorgeous hunk of man next to her in a photo while she smiled a satisfied smile and had perfect skin.

For now, she made herself another cup of tea, alone on a Sunday, and waited for her next online meeting. At least the virtual world was populated with those who still loved her.

· · · · · · · · · · · · · · · · · · ·

RULE #32 Only Princes are charming.
Grownup Kings have to be real.

· · · · · · · · · · · · · · · · · · ·

CHAPTER 20

PENISES

Artemisia went to the National Archaeological Museum. As she strolled through those elevated halls of art, she counted 42 visible penises in the first two rooms alone! Schlongs, wankers, willies, cocks, dicks. She pondered the fact they were such a taboo subject, but clearly it was not always so. These male models bared all; but, for a long time now, artistic renderings rarely exposed the frailties of our heroes. We didn't get to see Thomas Jefferson's John Thomas, for example. Or Lincoln's log. She laughed out loud despite herself. Penises came in all shapes and sizes—well, not really, a square one would be a bit awkward, but there's still a fair bit of variety. Straight, bent, usually one way but sometimes the opposite way or even a bit sideways. Big tips, little tips. Little tiny mushrooms and giant alien creatures from outer space. Smooth, veiny, pink, purple, brown, hairy, smooth. When they're soft even the biggest ones looked decidedly unimpressive. But women have thrown themselves off of bridges over them.

An absolute key ingredient in true, romantic love is sexual heat. It is the most seductive, beguiling, addictive thing in the universe, as much for women as for men, maybe even more so. We just weren't supposed to admit it. Losing a man you love, who sets off your rockets, was one of the hardest things in the world for a woman with a healthy drive, especially in her sexual prime. You could read all the psychology books, philosophize and even eulogize, but the detox period can be tough indeed. There are places people can go to get off drink and drugs, but when a woman misses a man's body, there is nowhere to go except to a shrink, to girlfriends, to the gym, but nothing really helps. There should be methadone clinic equivalents for this. Some women might go straight to another lover, but usually two great ones don't arrive back to back.

We've all seen the bitter woman who locks herself indoors after an ill-fated love affair or bad marriage. She seems to be a very old woman, no matter what her age. What is she missing? Scintillating conversation? Someone to help with the bills? Perhaps those too, but only real sexual passion can cause such sad regret, if a love affair was the cause.

Every day, in a million ways, breasts are being literally shoved in our faces, talked about, exploited, touted as the thing for a woman to have. But at the end of the day, the size of a woman's breasts do not directly impact sexual sensation as much as the size, shape and quality of the cock.

Not that bigger is always better. It's about the heat in the meat. How well a knight wields his sword, whether he is a 'cunning linguist,' his finesse, and if he is skilled in other ways. Making love, having sex, is a symphony of movements. It's not about pounding away like a jackhammer, whether you are big or small. Jackhammer sex is not good sex. Artemisia believed it was the result of too much porn, and not very good porn. It might also have some relationship to the type of music one listens to—admittedly, only a theory. She also believed it happened more with those on the other side of the neurobiological divide.

She also didn't like morning sex much. Mornings were her best time for thinking, writing, drinking coffee, starting her day. Sex was what you did in the middle for a tea break, or at the end. Morning sex, in her experience, was really for the man. She especially didn't like morning sex after a night of Jackhammer sex. Thankfully, she hadn't had much of that. In her experience, Aspies were sensitive, nuanced lovers. There seemed to be a kind of sexual savant quality that some had. Since hypersensitivity was now clinically recognized as part of autism, it made sense.

She stopped counting penises and just enjoyed the art.

. . . .

RULE #33 If you think you are a 'size queen' keep an open mind. It really is not the size of the baton, but the conductor who wields it.

. . . .

CHAPTER 21

GOOD GIRLS, BAD BOYS, JEALOUSY AND LOYALTY

In her travels, Artemisia met men who were faithful to their wives and girlfriends, and those who were not. Those who seemed to have a wholesome kind of soul and those who trod the darker paths. The latter were interesting to the single girl for two reasons: often they were skilled lovers as they've probably had more partners and practice. And they were a challenge: women like a challenge as much as a man does. For a man, the challenge might be getting and bedding a good girl. For a woman, it might be bagging a bad boy and getting him to put all his attentions on her, forsaking other women.

We might not know they're bad boys. Aspergirls are incredibly naive. When a man looked Artemisia directly in the eyes, she never thought, "He wants me," she just thought that he seemed like a friendly, open person.

Until now. Now, her own eyes were opening.

Lust was everywhere. It was veiled and hidden most of the time, but in some places, it was unveiled and unleashed. Trastevere after midnight, for example. Men looked past their long-suffering wives' shoulders as Artemisia approached, the flicker of a candle illuminating the unsated desires in their eyes.

She tried not to judge. No matter what feast you were fortunate enough to have been served by life, if you had to eat the same one every night, she supposed now and then you'd crave a pizza. Yet, when Artemisia loved someone, the way she had loved Rasputin, for example, she wanted only him. She couldn't stand the idea of someone else touching her. If she felt the need to stare at someone else like a dog looking at a bowl of food he knew wasn't his, then she'd probably end it.

She thought about how Rasputin and some of her dates like Caligulis gave each girl that crossed his path 'fuck me' eyes. She tolerated it because it took such a long time to realize what it was. She wondered if she would ever stop being so naive and trusting.

Part of the problem was that most Aspergirls don't really feel jealous of other women. If a woman is beautiful, we admire her. If she is smart or successful, we are proud of her. If she is happy, we can be happy for her. Today Artemisia had walked through Athens wearing fishnet stockings because she liked the way they felt and looked. Her nets ensnared dark looks from every corner. Tourists in loud American accents said "fishnets!" Women she knew scowled at her knees before recognizing her face. It was interesting the see the sudden shift of expression from judgment to "Oh, it's you!" Why judgmental? What was their reason? It had naught to do with her. What the hell was sexy about fishnets anyway?

Many women were jealous of her relationship with Rasputin. They were rude, bold, shameless. They would call him and invite him over when they knew she was there, living with him. She could not abide women being rude to other women over a man without just cause. If anything, she was protective of them. Women needed to band together the way that men did. She loved women, more than men, really. They were far more rational, capable, in so many ways. But she did not love them, unfortunately, for sex. If she did her story would be very different indeed. But for now, she had:

RULE #34 You might not be jealous or a cheater, but that doesn't make you immune to those who are.

CHAPTER 22

THE FRIEND ZONE

Artemisia hadn't seen Filos since the day Caligulis stood her up. As much as she liked him, she knew that he was not her type, for lots of reasons. The way he looked, dressed and she hated to say it, his physique. For her, physical fitness was an absolutely vital quality in a lover. She could be accused of discrimination or something, but we like what we like. Still, he was so nice and wanted to take her out dancing, so she decided to keep an open mind.

They were going clubbing. She did not club, although she liked to dance. She used to love it. They arrived at the first, seaside place. She hadn't even seen the Aegean yet apart from the airplane. She took a deep breath and jumped into the fray…well, descended the stairs into the land of the young and beautiful.

To her surprise it was pretty relaxed, fairly sophisticated. The music was not too loud to talk, the crowd was fairly grown up and well-dressed compared to what she was expecting. She couldn't help but look around. She didn't get out very often, really. Café and pub society are decidedly different from nightclub society. There was always an element of sexuality in clubs. Artemisia had a nice time although they didn't seem to have much to talk about. When they left and walked through the parking lot towards his car, Filos kissed her on the mouth. She cringed a little. She just didn't feel this way for him and was already wondering how to let him down kindly.

They went to Gazi, an area of Athens known for looking like a bomb hit it but also for all-night clubbing. Lines and lines of young people dressed in black, most with black hair, were everywhere waiting to get in somewhere. They parked on a street that looked like Armageddon had occurred there long ago. They arrived at a club he said he went to most nights. It became clear he knew all the staff, people who had that nighttime aura she'd become slightly unfamiliar with. When they entered she was hit with a physical wall of music that assaulted and repelled her. She flinched. It was not her age. This was supposed to be a date. There was no way one could have a conversation here. This place was a meat market. Why bring a date to a meat market? The music was pure video game. Filos kept shouting at her, telling her what the songs were about and dancing in place. There was no dance floor, just people standing around drinking and moving in their spot a little bit. Some girls writhed and wriggled on a balcony above. They did not look good, rather a bit like low price hookers on display. Artemisia felt sorry for them.

She could not hear a word Filos said unless he screamed into her ear while she had a finger in it to keep him from damaging her ear drum. There were strobe lights that she could not help but stare at. She could not focus on him so she looked around, and she noticed almost every young man in their vicinity was staring at her.

Filos asked, "Are you looking for someone or something?"

She replied honestly, "I'm a bit overwhelmed and don't know where or what to look at."

She did her best not to stare back at the other men, several of which were far more to her taste than her current companion. This was where she would go to get a toy boy, not be on a date.

He tried to kiss her again and she simply had to shout, "I don't feel that way about you, I'm sorry."

They left after one drink. She wanted to taxi home and let Filos try and salvage what was left of his night. She wouldn't have minded going to another club on her own, and finding someone a little more to her aesthetic taste to flirt with. In love and sex, aesthetics are important. While men and women fall in love all the time with people who are not their usual taste, there has to be a deep soul or intellectual compatibility. This was just a date and was never going to be anything more than that.

"What's wrong with you?" Filos asked.

She couldn't tell him her new rule, but she wanted to.

RULE #35 The word DATE should stand for 'Do All Things Effectively.'

Men: look at your date's attire, listen to her words, read her body language. If she is really into you, you can take her almost anywhere, but if she's on the fence, it's all riding on your next choice. If she looks horrified at the entrance of a place, take her somewhere else. Or not...it's up to you.

Artemisia felt that, despite his generosity and gentlemanly behavior, it was still a little selfish of him to take her there. He wanted to show her off at his regular hangout. And it was not the first time a man did that: took her someplace where everyone knew him, as if to show off his 'catch of the day.'

. . . .

RULE #36 You are not there to make someone else look good, you are there to enjoy *your* life, don't forget your own importance. So,

. . . .

. . . .

RULE #37 Don't meet your date's friends until you know if you like him or her well enough— and that takes time—or you'll feel vulnerable.

. . . .

Age was not the real issue here, it was sophistication. Her 22-year-old Roman knew what Filos did not. Leonardo took her for dinner, and a quiet walk by the river, told her she was *bellissima*, then kissed her passionately. The last time she had been on a date here in Gazi, it was with an older gentleman. Although she was in a long, fancy evening dress, he brought her to a cheap restaurant where tattooed and purple-haired art school kids proceeded to laugh indiscreetly at her. Tonight she was dressed perfectly for Gazi, but still…

She couldn't expose herself to five hours of 'what he wants' without a bit of what she wanted just because he was buying her a couple of drinks. After all, she spent a lot more money on clothes, hair, makeup and time on getting ready than he did, and that is almost always the case on heterosexual dates. Dates are expensive—for women!

People forget how much preparation can go into a date. Women buy shoes, outfits, expensive perfume and makeup, even for the most standard of rendezvous. Whether you shop at H&M or Gucci, it's probably still a sizable investment according to your income. Even if you are mega-rich and he's a stockboy, he should pay, unless you are insisting on top floor hotel bar and champagne while he has a cold can of beer in the park budget. Therefore,

RULE #38 Women should (almost) never pay on heterosexual dates. You are setting a precedent. If you are partners, that's a different story.

And, lastly, she supposed that on some level she used Filos to get out on the weekend and have something to do. And now she felt bad about it. She valued their budding friendship, which she felt fairly certain, was fucked. He really was a sweet person. He didn't even laugh at her when she poked herself in the eye with the straw when she went to take a drink— twice! Good ol' Aspergers and those spatial awareness issues. Maybe, over time, they would be friends again. She hoped so.

RULE #39 Keep friends in the friend zone.

While starting out as friends is the best, you have to be sure if and when you feel differently about them, so you don't risk losing a valuable relationship.

CHAPTER 23

EVERYTHING IS BIGGER IN TEXAS

Artemisia was on the way to *Street Wok*, for delicious cheap eats like she used to make at home, without having to wash up afterwards. Plus they played good tunes while you waited for your takeaway. She bumped into Nina, a casual acquaintance who happened to be on her way to a singing gig in a restaurant.

Nina convinced Artemisia that her presence was needed this night, so she agreed to come.

She sat, she listened and was enraptured at Nina's agile vocals and the liquid sound of the bazouki. She ordered wine and food and sat comfortably in the manner of a world-traveled writer. She'd seen it in films.

There was a group of international conference attendees tearing up the dance floor like a giant version of the Village People except not ostensibly gay. One of them caught Artemisia's eye. First, they danced, not very well, not very badly. Then they spoke; there was chemistry. Jack was a normal, attractive, witty American from Texas. He seemed nice, not at all like a player or serial charmer. Artemisia liked him. He asked her to meet him at his hotel bar, her favorite, for it had one of the best views in the city. She knew she would go to his room, unless he blew it.

She went home and changed, because she was dressed for noodles, not for champagne, which is what she told him to order. When she arrived in the lobby of the hotel, all of his conference mates were there. They looked at her funny, like she had followed them. She felt a bit like a hooker, but she didn't know why. Women met men for drinks at bars all the time. This was normal adult behavior, wasn't it?

He was drinking scotch and already a bit more drunk than she'd like, but the view was exquisite and his manners and wit had not abandoned him. They kissed. It was surprisingly good.

They took their second glass to his room. There had been no one since Caligulis and Artemisia was still on a mission to experience life and to keep herself from dwelling in the past.

When he undressed, she was taken aback. "Wow, I guess everything *is* bigger in Texas." She hadn't seen anything quite like that in *years*.

His body was willing but she could tell he seemed a little reticent.

"You've just broken up with someone haven't you?" she asked.

"Yes, a few months ago."

"And I'm the first one since?" Of course, transitional girl.

She enjoyed it even if she could feel him thinking. Maybe this was why she liked young, less complicated men: less mental distraction. By 4 or 5AM she knew she should leave but she was exhausted and, frankly, she wanted to be held. She couldn't get him to do that so she had sex with him again. But this time he had no care for her needs, her satisfaction. He came, rolled over and went back to sleep. Finally, dawn arrived.

She said "That was fun...*ciao*," and left, clutching hotel soaps under her arms.

She didn't like that he got unnecessarily cold. Why did men do that? Did women? She hadn't been with enough females to remember. She was not falling in love with Jack. She liked him. It was a fun night and that was it. She felt nothing afterward. No emotion, just...cool. It did not leave her feeling attached, let down, or wanting more. Maybe because he was going to India that very day.

As far as she was concerned, Jack could have stayed pleasant and charming the way he had been and the memory of the night would have been perfect. If she could have the sexual pleasure from a one night stand that she did from a long-term relationship, she'd probably keep doing it. No guilt, no depending on—or having to answer to—another person. No responsibilities toward the happiness and wellbeing of another. She saw now the allure and possibly the danger...or was it simply the ultimate freedom?

. . . .

RULE #40 People will get cold after a one night stand to avoid giving off the relationship vibe if they don't want one. You might feel it's unnecessary but it's a pretty common defense mechanism.

. . . .

CHAPTER 24

ASPIE ANXIETY AND THAT DAMN GLOW

Artemisia spent the morning meeting 'her people' at a clinic in Athens. She may have passed as an outwardly social, even highly social being at times, but today she was reminded that she was an Aspie. After the delightful meeting with half a dozen young, very Aspie males and one girl, she went out for a drink with her psychologist friend, Alethea, who'd arranged it all. Artemisia went home feeling fine, did some work and then Alethea invited her to yoga.

Her old social burnout was nowhere to be seen. She accepted. Then, Alethea casually dropped, "You will meet my friends."

Screech. Her hard drive ground to a halt. She could not do it. She was not up for a new class, a new environment, in a new neighborhood…with new people to talk to. They will no doubt have heard good things about her that she did not feel she could live up to. Artemisia was not in the mood to be scrutinized, even gently. She felt so bad about it that she wanted to cry. She knew that if she went she would feel awkward and Alethea would wonder what happened to the outgoing, colorful woman she had been getting to know.

She stayed in Plaka, the most boring area of Athens, but also the most beautiful. She needed the familiar faces of her local bartenders, baristas, waiters, wranglers (the ones that lured the customers in off the streets) and neighbors. She craved the sight of the nameless cats that roamed the area or curled up in potted plants. She needed the golden lights of Acropolis to enfold her in their warmth. Artemisia had Anxiety.

She bumped into Nina on her walk, who once more invited her to her gig. "We had so much fun last time, but you left…"

"Another night, I promise."

She was comfortable with her decision. A bit sad, but we can't fight our nature, not all the time, anyway.

She decided to write, but at least to do so in a café. She chose a new place, younger and hipper than the tavernas which surrounded it. Filled with trepidation, she entered alone and sat at the bar with her laptop, surrounded by enough staff to attend a whole restaurant filled with people. There was only her. The food was delicious, and she just began to relax, when she dropped her knife on the floor with the loudest clatter imaginable…of course she did. Whenever she felt vulnerable, fate made certain to make something happen to bring her unwanted attention.

"I didn't do it, some man jumped in the window, knocked it off the table and ran away."

They laughed kindly. She was once again convinced that Greece, if you were willing to put a smile on your face even when you didn't necessarily feel like it, was the best place to be an Aspie.

She ended up having a long private conversation with the manager, Frakas. He was fluent in English but, more than that, he was clever. They had many of the same likes and dislikes, in drinks, culture, music, TV, film. They talked nonstop for hours. She drank a little more than she knew she should, but her apartment door was only 50 meters away so again she was comfortable with her choices.

Around midnight, she said "This was fun," and left feeling delighted.

It was so nice to find you had so many things in common with someone from the other side of the world. She'd tried not to seem too interested in this man. She wasn't sure if she was, in any sense other than a buddy to talk to. But Greek men, and indeed, men from many other cultures (Italians definitely excluded), made it difficult to find out. She'd spoken to many Greek women, and they all told her the same thing—Greek men didn't flirt. Unless it was 2AM and dark and everyone was drunk. But those were not the best conditions to meet someone, even Artemisia knew that. From what she could gather, oftentimes men wouldn't show they were interested, but when you walked away they'd stare after you. Her married friends were pretty good at flirting, but they were in the 'safe zone' as far as she was concerned. Like they were just making sure they still got it, from the safe bosoms of their marriages.

Artemisia was an open book; too open. More like an opened map. When she liked talking to someone, she was animated. When she really liked them, whether it was just friendship or more, she'd glow like that damn creature in *Stardust*. She came home and looked in the mirror. Damn it. She was glowing. Frakas must know she's interested. She couldn't feign interest or disinterest in someone. If she liked them, she liked them. This was why only the men she didn't want, wanted her. They saw her disinterest. This piqued their need for the chase.

Men needed the chase. They want to bed the good girl, the one that's hard to get. Women also need the chase, or at least this woman. They want to bed the bad boy and keep him there. Both of these are fraught with illusion and difficulty.

Looking back at all the dates she'd had over the last three months, they were all with men that she did not have an initial reaction to, other than, 'oh look, it's a human.' Even tonight, she could have had three dates, but they were all with the ones she DIDN'T want. The one she did...nothing. That's it! She must learn to feign disinterest. Damn, this world is so complicated. She felt yet another migraine coming on. She was convinced they were from lack of someone to hold. As awful as her last relationship was, every night they held each other tightly in their sleep, shared the same breath. They were close. That is, if and when he came home. She glanced in the mirror as she brushed her teeth and readied herself for bed...still glowing. Damn Aspergers. She'd convince herself that she was not interested so that next time she saw him, she wouldn't glow like a light saber and be twice as scary.

. . . .

RULE #41 Try not to get overexcited and rehearse wedding vows in your head the moment you meet someone you like.

. . . .

You don't know anything about them and they don't know anything about you.

CHAPTER 25

TRAVEL, TRADITIONS AND TRANSITIONS

Travel, transitions, change were all difficult for Artemisia for many reasons, both directly and indirectly related to her Aspergers. Having to get to an airport alone with all that luggage; what to do if a flight is delayed or canceled; being in countries where you don't speak or read the language. So many variables, maybe you didn't bring the right clothes. And other perhaps more vague unspecific worries, such as "will I ever see this place again?"

But then there was the anonymity of travel. How she did love that sometimes. And of course the way she felt each time she saw something new, something of special magnificence and beauty. When she caught her first glimpse of the marble columns and grand statues of Vatican City, she uttered aloud "holy fuck" and then covered her mouth apologetically as two nuns passed.

There was the education it provided to even the most intellectually lazy or passive people. She learned far more about French life and culture after three months in Paris than she could ever learn in a classroom. Although, of course, the latter would have given her some language, background and history and would have been far less disillusioning.

There is strength imparted to a person who travels alone. You are tested. And there are spiritual elements to each place, Artemisia firmly believed that. She had much to be grateful to Athens for. It was there and there only she found the strength to leave a life that didn't work, to search for one that might, even if she hadn't quite found it yet.

She told all her friends, "You must visit. But there are things to know about the Greeks. They won't wear sandals until May no matter how hot it gets. You can wear sleeveless tops and mini-skirts but if they see sight of a toenail you might as well be walking down the street naked from the disapproving stares.

They wear down-filled parkas when it's 80°F (27°C). And wool scarves. And heavy boots. The American tourists are running around in shorts and tees getting suntans and the Greeks look like they are going Christmas shopping.

They are a superstitious people, the Christians as much if not more so than the pagans. Everything is caused by 'The Eye.' Have a migraine? It's because men are staring at you thinking bad thoughts. Say *ftou ftou* to prevent it next time. Have a stomach ache? Someone gave you The Eye. Call your grandmother and she will say a prayer/cast a spell and it will be all better.

And they *are* loud. It is not a cliché and they are the first to admit it. Bring earplugs!"

That was the source of at least some of her frequent migraines. Her favorite high decibel encounter was with a dermatologist she met after being roped in off the street for a free consultation.

"How you think you look?" yelled the lab-coated professional from three feet away, as if Artemisia were on the other side of the Aegean.

"Good," Artemisia replied, smiling confidently yet warily.

"No!" She yelled even louder. "You don't! Your face is *empty.*"

The last word was said with great emphasis, her look carefully crafted to strike terror into the heart and cause a person to scream for her to inject their empty face with anything. Artemisia should have run out the door but the loud volume worked like a stun gun, and she was rooted to her chair for another hour before the 2000 euro price estimate pried her ass up and out of there. But, truth is, she liked the woman. She liked most of the people she met there, even Dr. Frankenscream.

The Greeks were loud but they were also friendly, unpretentious, nice to talk to, and affectionate. Maybe Artemisia hadn't been kissed on the lips much, but she'd been kissed on the cheek more times in three months than both her grandmothers ever did put together. She genuinely loved these people. She would be back, she knew it.

She had two new best girlfriends, much like those she met in Rome, who felt like old friends, like she'd known them forever. Neither of them, unlike the ones in Rome, were on the spectrum. (There was less of a divide here it seemed.) But romance, that was a different story. In a few days she'd go back to the states for the first time in six months. "Greek men, I am leaving. You have missed your chance," she would yell from the rooftops, but they wouldn't seem bothered.

Tonight she asked Frakas, point blank: "Come home with me."

"I like having Artemisia as a friend and that would change," he said.

"Yes, it would be even better," she argued, but he wouldn't budge.

She didn't feel humiliated...much.

She went to her local and spoke to Heracles, a handsome if slightly off-putting young man.

"I'm writing a book," she said "and I need some insight into Greek men, if not men in general."

"We want to be the one to initiate," he told her. "We think that if a woman has to ask, there must be something wrong with her."

"That's so outdated," she told him, "and silly."

"Yes, but that's the way it is."

If she waited for a man to ask her out, at least in most countries, she would be dead before it happened. Was it like this everywhere? In Italy, they move fast. Her Italian suitors came at her so quickly she didn't have a chance to ask. In fact, now that she thought about it, the ones she did blatantly make the moves on were a little put off. Hmmm. So, with this logic, she had to live in a place where men were comfortable flirting, which might mean that they wouldn't make solid partners. Sigh. So complicated.

When she got back to her flat, she cried for Rasputin for the first time in a long time. As much as she knew he was a giant turd, he never turned down any woman for sex and was good for that in his way, what the French called *un coq*. If only he had been honest with her from the beginning, instead of promising true love, and shown her who he truly was, perhaps they would have been just friends...with benefits.

Well, at least she had:

. . . .

RULE #42 Men must be the first ones to make a blatant move (if it's men you want).

. . . .

Otherwise they will think you're either easy or there's something wrong with you. This realization made her feel as if she'd fallen into a past century. And here she was, thinking she lived in a fairly non-sexist world all this time. So many blindfolds were falling from her eyes, and so quickly, she was afraid they might get burned from seeing the light so strongly for the first time.

CHAPTER 26

CONTRADICTIONS AND CHOICE

The next day she went for a haircut. The man took four inches off, instead of the half inch she'd asked for. After what Heracles said, it left her feeling doubly disempowered. She felt like a slave to a man's fancy, to age, to circumstance.

"If you want to meet a man, go to a club," some people told her.

"You will never meet a good man in a club," others said.

"Men go after what they want."

"Men don't make the first move."

Contradictions, contradictions. All she knew for certain was that she was losing that feeling of being sensual and beautiful without someone to keep that fire stoked.

Something about Athens made everything come into clearer focus, even illuminating that which was not in focus yet, but needed to be. She learned about friends, having them, being one. She learned that she was in a bad relationship, even if she did not yet clearly know what a good one would be like.

She was going back to see her family in two days. She'd learned that family would try to pull you back to the past, and guilt trip you into doing things. But instead of cutting them out of your life, like she often did in the past, it was better to establish boundaries. And give them the opportunity to develop some new strategies themselves. Those ties could not be severed by time or space.

Life is often one long succession of disempowering situations—hairdressers who ignore our wishes, people who shun us, flights in which we are strapped into our seats with no control over anything, banks, the tax man. Everything in life seems to conspire to take our choices and decisions away from us. Even learning can be disempowering. We acquire knowledge from teachers who tell us "This is the way." Still, we can choose whether to believe it, act on it, adopt it as our own belief system, or walk away.

To remember we have freedom of choice in life is perhaps one of the most difficult things but maybe the most important. Maybe this is why people choose to color their hair, get tattoos. To have some sort of control over the lottery of life. Some people have babies because this too, gives us a sort of godlike ability—the power to create life.

But there in the land of the Gods, Artemisia remembered from her mythology books how even they made bad choices and unwise decisions. It was a risk we all must take and there were never any guarantees that things would work out the way we wanted. She felt frustrated but empowered, knowing that nothing or no one she'd encountered, had made her its ideological slave. This whole adventure started because she left what she loved most in the world. She had to for her own survival. Once you did that, it became easier to spot and leave unhealthy situations before they hurt you.

. . . .

RULE #43 Don't blindly adhere to any love or philosophy, only to the power of Choice.

. . . .

CHAPTER 27

THE MARRIED MUSLIM

It was Artemisia's last night here in Athens and she'd said all her important goodbyes, save one. She was meeting Stavros for a drink. He owned a company and was probably her only friend with real money. He taught her things he thought she ought to know, and sometimes he was right. Other times he was a bit pedantic and well, male, but she always tried to listen to him with an open mind.

They were at Benetti's, a local meeting place that made her favorite drink, a fizzy lemon. Tonight she was followed and courted on the street for several blocks by a young man, who was good-natured when she told him that he could be a thief for all she knew and she wasn't going to tell him her name. She was learning.

Now at Benetti's Artemisia was being stared at by the usual handsome bad boy. She stared back for a moment. She could have him if she wanted. This was easier than she thought. Why couldn't she do this in her twenties—or for the last month for that matter? Stavros shook his head in despair.

"You need to find someone with money to help take care of you and treat you to the lush life. Or at least a more comfortable one."

"OK. I'll see if something better arrives." She wanted to find out if she had the confidence to handle their attention… that is, if she got it.

In walked Thurston Howell the fourth and his friend, Biff Biffington of the Connecticut Biffingtons. They looked like they just stepped off of a yacht—Daddy's yacht.

Not to her taste at all, but just to annoy Stavros, she said, "What about that?"

He scoffed and before she had a chance to say 'only joking,' immediately two men entered, dark, tall, confident.

"Now, that's money," said Stavros. "They aren't putting on any airs."

One of them looked right at Artemisia and she looked back, their eyes locked for a moment. She would never have looked at him twice if it weren't for Stavros' rather aggressive coaching.

"Put down your drink and walk over there. I will pretend to be your gay friend."

That wouldn't be difficult considering he had a toy poodle in a pink sweater in a pink carrying case with him.

She walked past the two men to the ladies room. In Greece, all toilets shared a unisex outer door. Within moments he walked in, said hello. They began to chat but it smelled like a toilet, definitely not the right ambience.

"Why don't you join us?" she asked him.

It took ages for the stranger to come out and she wondered if he were afraid or ill, or both, but eventually he did and the two men joined them. His friend bought their drinks with a black Mastercard—the kind that had no limits—so she didn't feel bad when she sent hers back.

"Absinthe does not always make the heart grow fonder," she jokingly told her new friend.

They talked about all the basic things: where do you live, what do you do, that sort of thing.

"Married?" she asked. She remembered this time. Progress.

"Of course."

"Kids?"

"Yep, I was Skyping with them just now."

Ah, so it wasn't dysentery keeping him so long in the bathroom then. Well, that was good to know.

He had to respond to a question from his friend but as he turned away, his hand gently cupped her cheek. It was so intimate and would normally have upset if not repelled her. But he had such a sensual way about him it seemed quite natural. Stavros and the other man chatted about international finance and other things that would have bored Artemisia to tears. She liked this man. He was intelligent, eloquent, a gentleman, and he clearly liked her.

"The passion has gone out of my marriage a little and it's making me sad."

She saw real concern in his eyes, nostalgia as opposed to blame or disinterest. Artemisia had never been with a married man, but she felt like she might not be able to stop herself, if he weren't leaving for Dubai and she weren't leaving for New York, both in a matter of hours.

"Do you have anyone in NY pulling you back?"

"Yes, my daughter." Artemisia felt like she was betraying Elle if she denied her.

Then, of course, the look on his face said, *Why aren't you with her?*

To which she had to reply, "She's grown up." She lied a little and made Elle a tiny bit younger. When she saw the surprise on his face, she had to brag, "and she has a baby."

"You're a grandmother?" he asked, clearly astonished.

"I don't use that word, we use 'Ama,'" and then she immediately felt weird.

"We have to get up at 4AM for a flight," he said a bit later and moved as if to go. "How can I get in touch with you?"

She had no card with her. "Google me."

He left.

Stavros was sending his driver to take her to the airport at 10AM but she woke up unhappily at 6AM. Something was bothering her. She realized suddenly, with perfect hindsight, all the various things she did wrong.

RULE #44 Don't send your drink back. It's not about the drink, it's about the conversation.

RULE #45 Don't volunteer anything that is less than flattering.

You might be the sexiest grandmom in the world but frankly it's still not sexy and should be reserved for more established relationships.

RULE #46 Give him your number or at least an email if you want to hear from him.

Googling someone is either going to be a difficult job if you aren't well-known, or its going to be a scare fest if you are and there are lots of unflattering pics and even birthdates on there.

She was now left wondering if her new crush would write. He said he'd remember her name and seemed sincere but, to this Aspie, *didn't they all?*

Artemisia learned one thing for sure, that despite the challenges that age and Aspergers entailed, the light that shone in her and others like her was still attractive to those who had eyes to see. The problem was that some of those were exotic gentlemen with manners and money, and others were malignant narcissists, and everyone in between and she still wasn't the best judge of character. She kind of wished she had Stavros with her every time she met a potential date. Maybe she should start shooting short videos of potential candidates and sending them to him. She guessed that could be one of the benefits of online dating; having a video that you can study as some of them do, and showing it to a trusted friend.

Her plane was landing soon. When she returned to her house in Western NY, she would have six weeks to find out for surely there would be no other way to meet someone there on the edge of nowhere.

CHAPTER 28

THE VIRTUAL LIFE

There in Buffalo and the outskirts where Artemisia still technically lived, she historically had not had much luck meeting men. Her last home-grown squeeze was the guy that mowed her lawn, a constellation of oft-perplexing traits who turned out to be the Aspie that set her on the path of self-discovery and a career as an author. So, while not a total loss, romantically, nothing came out of it that she could look back on with terrible fondness.

This was a small town and since her daughter was older than her last lovers, there was bound to be some talk, some raised eyebrows and a few 'good-natured' insults. Between trips to Europe, she'd dated or hung out with a couple of Elle's male friends and the girl was not amused. Artemisia tried to walk the line between not embarrassing her daughter and living the life she wanted. But, as it turned out, we were all an embarrassment to our children anyway. Elle was now married with a baby of her own. The days of behaving for the PTA were a thing of the past. She had a book to write, and a life to live.

But she knew the pickings there...slim if not nonexistent. So she filled out her first online profile in the last decade, on a site dedicated to matching women of humble means with men of substantial means. If she was going to go out of character, she might as well go all the way. Meanwhile, Ken, a friend of Elle's that had long had some kind of chaste crush on Artemisia, began his usual empty flirt whenever she was in town. Now that she'd had men like Leonardo, she no longer felt the need to be grateful just because she had the eye of the best looking man in Buffalo. What mattered was, could they have a conversation that didn't bore her to tears? Were they going to stay beyond the morning? Could they make her laugh? Feel good about herself? Set off her rockets? Could they fit in with the lifestyle she'd become accustomed to? The international way of life suited her. Everyone said so.

Her first attempt at a profile was rejected as 'too explicit.' What? She said 'uninhibited sex.' That's explicit? Welcome to the land founded by people so prudish they were kicked out of all the fun countries. Happiness came from within, but it's definitely made easier by outside circumstances—being in a place and around people that 'ping' the inner happiness in you, instead of repelling it and causing it to crawl into a cave and hide.

She finished her profile and the next morning woke to 29 views and four messages. All four said exactly the same thing: "Hi."

"You had one chance to make a first impression and you filled it with 'Hi?'" she shouted at her computer. Clearly this was not going to work for her.

She went to meet a friend of her daughter's (who was also now a friend of hers), Misha, in Elmwood, the trendy heart of Buffalo, a city on the west end of NY state. Walking toward The Pink on Allen Street (a place that truly made her feel like an ageless vampire, as she'd been going for decades and was always presumed to be a newbie) she heard "How you doin'?" from a group of passing youths. She supposed it was the Buffalo version of *bellissima* and, while not as exotic, it was still nice.

Misha and she had a lot in common despite the age and neurological differences. A beautiful young woman, she was just abruptly unfriended by her lover, an eastern European teacher with whom she'd had a passionate affair. She needed to talk about it with someone who understood the withdrawal pains of passion lost. Artemisia told her not to look for happiness in a man but Misha was one step ahead of her. She'd already wished him well and was recovering swiftly. She knew instinctively what many Aspies did not.

. . . .

RULE #47 Love was supposed to make you feel good.

. . . .

Aspies are so used to feeling odd and uncomfortable we don't really have the capacity to understand that right away, sometimes we never do.

CHAPTER 29

THE AMERICAN BOY

It was a great sad irony that she was far more attractive to handsome twenty-somethings now than she ever was in her twenties. In fact she was perhaps more beautiful now, with confidence she never remotely possessed before.

A handsome young man with a crew cut was playing darts with his friends. She liked the way that they were warm and affectionate with each other—people were not like this when she came here decades ago. The damn punk era. He caught her eye, she caught his. They spoke. Mark was from a classic, big, Irish family. He'd never traveled out of the US before, but was excited about an upcoming trip to Asia. She told him what she knew about it. He was impressed with her world knowledge, especially because he clearly thought she was his age. They talked closely, held hands, went for a walk, kissed. He was smitten.

"What did I do to deserve the most beautiful woman around?"

Hours later, she left an understanding Misha sipping gin cocktails and making new friends at The Pink, and took Mark to her van. They spread out her foldaway mattress which she'd bought for music touring, which, in her naivete, she never even imagined would be used for sex. Until now, it never had been.

Sometimes, soft and dry is good, like when you are talking about towels or blankets. When talking about other things, well, not so good. Mark couldn't get hard. Clearly he adored her, and was quite comfortable with his body and infatuated with hers. He simply could not get hard.

It's a fact that some men were, on some level, shy of the one night stand. It was not the first time she encountered this phenomenon. Usually she saw the man again and the second time it was all engines go, but first time, it might as well be Groundhog day in January. Punxsutawney Phil was not raising his head. What did they do? Everything they could. Did she get upset? No. When she was younger, she would have been very upset. She would have thought that it was some fault of hers that she wasn't sexually proficient or attractive enough. She would have melted down and sulked, yelled or cried.

It might be hard to understand how Aspergers affected her life and indeed her sex life. She remembered a day long ago, she was alone in a restaurant in Manhattan. There was a window she wanted to look out of so she went and sat next to it. Unfortunately there was already a group of people sitting at that table. She didn't realize it was inappropriate for her to do this. She was 22 years old. Needless to say, men did not line up back then to take her out.

These last months she dated five young men in their twenties. In her own twenties, she'd dated two. Then she got engaged to an older man, one that she didn't love, thinking she was ready to have a normal, middle-aged life. She never had a proper young adulthood. She was having it now.

Mark wanted to see her again but of course, she knew that wasn't a good idea. When she went out to her van the next morning to survey the mess and tidy up, she found his car key, so it appeared she had no choice. She couldn't just throw it away, that would be cruel. He had given her his number, so she took a deep breath and called him: it went straight to voicemail. The phone must be dead, or maybe lost. She imagined it falling into a gutter next to her van, still there in a trickle of filthy rain water and remnants of dead winter leaves. She would have wanted to see him again, but 21 was too young. She imagined Stavros shaking his head and sighing, but there was something so irresistible in those fresh blue eyes, the vintage crewcut, the hillbilly harmonica ringtone on his now missing phone. Why could she not have this in her youth? To experience the sweetness, the tenderness, the soft skin and firmness of a beautiful young man was, to her, still one of the greatest pleasures on earth.

Finally she reached him. He would come later, around 6 he said.

"My brother will have to bring me."

She came alive with anticipation, imagined him being dropped off for a night of passion to make up for the opportunity lost the night before. She'd take him to work herself the next morning, or he would get picked up by an obliging relative or coworker.

The car pulled into the drive. Another gorgeous brother. She'd already met one at The Pink the night before. Mark had come straight from work, smelling of construction and sweat, looking completely different in the wicked light of day, the vintage crewcut now looking strictly utilitarian. The magic was gone.

"Can I see you again sometime?" he asked, with no indication he wanted that time to be now.

"I don't think so," she smiled sweetly and closed the door on yet another silly dream.

. . . .

RULE #48 They don't have to be illegal to be too young.

. . . .

. . . .

RULE #49 Alcohol, moonlight and music makes almost everyone seem more attractive.

. . . .

. . . .

RULE #50 If you are going to meet a lover—past present or future—don't kill the magic, clean yourself up!

. . . .

CHAPTER 30

BRON

Bron was, quite simply, the gayest straight man she had ever met. Slender, soft-spoken, preoccupied with clothes. She met him in her son-in-law Rico's garage. She burst in, stole a cigarette, said a few things and left.

Rico told her later Bron asked, "Where can I get one of those?"

To which he replied, "You can't, dude, she's unique."

The next weekend she was van-camping as she often did when she rented out her house to holiday-makers. She used it as an excuse to go partying in Buffalo's Allentown, the bar district. First, she popped into Elle's rehearsal, proudly saw her daughter sing, surrounded by sinewy musicians that were in Elle's thrall, then afterward ran into Bron again at Elle's house. They all agreed to meet at Nietzsche's, an ancient mainstay in the Allentown district near Elmwood and, from there, made the rounds. All roads in Elmwood lead to The Pink, which is where Rico stole Bron's car and left, effectively dumping him into Artemisia's lap. She'd had a few drinks so, by American legal standards, was unfit to drive, and she certainly couldn't just leave him on the street. At 4AM almost everyone can be to anyone's taste, so she found herself dirty dancing him up against a wall at the aptly named Hardware Cafe.

They went to her van and, much to her amazement, not only was Bron straight, but his size and his wild hunger were in direct contrast to his thin body and mild manner. He had been celibate for a year. Lucky Artemisia—in fact, he ravaged her like a savage artist. Not only did she orgasm but she yelled uncontrollably while it was happening. Perhaps it was the alcohol but she had virtually no brakes on herself at the moment.

He was the best and most surprising lover she had since Rasputin. Committed (to the moment), kind, compassionate, seemingly intelligent; but, unlike Rasputin, still very innocent. And unfortunately, too unripe to forge any kind of real relationship.

In the morning they got lattes and went for a walk in the rain.

She had to drive him to get his car. On the way, they stopped to take a nap at one of the many little parks on the shore of Lake Erie heading out of the city. In the parking lot she pulled the curtains. The whoosh of skateboards made a sort of serenade. They did it again, held each other tight, slept a bit. She really liked this one. He was a special sweet young man.

They met again the following weekend and it was almost as good as the first time and nearly as surprising. But where could it go? They looked ridiculous together. And anyway, soon she would be leaving for Rome. She was terrified of travel. She was a dragon, a bull and an Aspie. The dragon wanted to soar, the bull wanted to stay put, while the Aspie was convinced she would die in a fiery plane crash. She invited

Bron to spend her last night with her, at her home, so she wouldn't be so afraid. He'd never been there before and she liked the idea of enjoying him properly in a comfy bed with a kitchen and bathroom nearby, instead of on a tiny futon in a cramped space with no running water.

She would miss him, but who knows? Maybe he'd come to see her in Rome. Surely a man with so much passion for sex would embrace a romantic journey like the one she would offer.

"Let me read your tarot," she suggested. She hoped it would provide encouragement.

The cards were all about a crush on a woman, but there were some problems. Despite strong feelings, words were getting in the way.

"Oh, you have a crush on someone?" she smirked, knowing full well he did.

"Well, there *is* this girl at work," he replied.

"I see," was all she could say. Transitional girl.

Her last night in New York, she slept alone. It was better this way.

The nights she left Paris, she and Rasputin would stay up all night, mostly talking, but of course it was Paris so there would always be wine, and it was Rasputin so there would always be sex. Whether it was tender or not, sober or not, late night, early morning, whether they were having one of their close days or feeling distant, it was never just sex—it was always making love. She hated to leave and he hated her to leave, despite what he would later tell half of France. He was a master of spin and deception. Parting was always traumatic. But it had to be done. And, the last time, it had to be done for good.

So far, love had just been illusion followed by a period of enduring a brutal shattering of illusion, no matter how hard she tried to keep it alive—it could only become a gruesome caricature of itself, like a creature in Pet Sematary.

The tattoo that she got at 15 now held more truth than ever. She had a winged heart. And once again it had to fly... this time, back to Rome.

. . . .

RULE #51 Freedom is equal to love,
and superior to unhealthy love.

. . . .

CHAPTER 31

WRITER'S BLOCK

She walked past his café: he was there. Leonardo saw her, but Artemisia kept walking. She rounded the block and came at his place from the other side. She entered. He looked up… they beamed at each other. Clear affection. They hugged, he spoke in Italian and broken English; she, the opposite. Leonardo was thin, too thin. She was almost shocked by it.

"Doesn't your girlfriend feed you?" she asked sarcastically.

"Yes, but I don't sleep enough," he said.

She knew that.

"I am going to Scotland," he told her. "With my girlfriend."

"The same one?" she asked, to which he nodded.

"When are you getting married?"

"No!" He replied emphatically, "I only 22."

"Yes, but you are traveling together."

"Next time I travel alone," he said, "to Athens."

So many times she wanted to invite him and now she found out he had been entertaining the same thoughts. He wanted to come. She was too excited to see him, she could not stop herself from beaming. The other staff (Raffaele and his Gomez 'tache were gone), including some woman who had that disapproving look Artemisia couldn't stand, were all watching closely. They all looked as if they feared Artemisia and Leonardo would pounce on each other at any moment and they'd have to pull them apart. The attraction *was* palpable. He used her translator. She touched his hands lightly with her fingertips. She was dying to reach up and stroke his almost full beard. His hair still looked like he belonged in the seventies. She must go. If she drank a second glass of wine, at worst she'd make an ass of herself; at best, she would be too tired for him later. For he was coming over when the restaurant closed.

She left floating on air and headed in no particular direction, except she had a vague realization that it was not towards home. After a few minutes, she spied a man coming her way, who, like a lot of Romans, made bold eye contact and said, *"Buona sera."*

She said "hi" and kept walking. Ten paces later she turned around to find that he'd turned around too. She smiled but continued on. A moment later he sidled up alongside her. Normally this would really creep her out but he looked like he stepped out of a Botticelli painting and she couldn't resist. He asked a couple of basic questions, she responded with one of her own:

"Buy me a drink?"

They sat at a shoddy place she used to sometimes go to write during the day and which now had the rattle, hum and stench of a night time scene. Sandro was a writer too, published, cute. But she was tired, a little bored. She wondered "What is wrong with me?" and thought of kissing him just to get her heart rate going so she could keep awake.

Finally, she said, "I must go."

"Go where?" he asked.

"On a date."

"Have a date with me," he replied.

Okay, first of all, he was much more age- and occupation-appropriate than her Leonardo. Second of all, he was nice and very handsome. Third, she knew from experience that the worst thing she could do would be to let a man know that he was indispensable to her. No one was. Men who were attracted to her, men like Rasputin, would take that information and use it to commit every crime known to exist—against love, against humanity, and most importantly, against her.

So she said, "Why not?" and messaged Leonardo that she could not see him tonight, that she ran into some friends.

Sandro's apartment was very close, mere steps away. It had been in his family for years and had an un-ironic retro feel, with lots of 70s browns and oranges, big clunky furniture, and wood and glass overhead lamps. He showed her the novels he wrote and verbally listed all the books he'd been reading. Maybe he wanted to impress her, or to discuss those books, but she never read anything anymore—too busy living and writing. Maybe she should. They had some rum and went to his bed.

Under this man's body, she felt like a bowlful of butter under the tongue of a dog. So much tongue, so much spit. Not enough penis. His tongue was not gentle and probing the way she liked, the way she felt fairly certain most women liked, but instead it was like a giant fish shoved into her mouth, the way that many of these Romans kissed. Someone, somewhere, started a very strange tradition. Probably one of those deranged Caesars. Meanwhile, down below, there wasn't a lot going on. What was it that happened to young men, that made them lose the ability to get hard? He was only 32.

"Sorry, this has been happening for a while. I have lost my rhythm."

So, it was not her. She mused that when the brain interfered with the libido, or when the libido interfered too much with the brain, one ceased to live a healthy life. The man talked almost ceaselessly about the books he read and, while it was a welcome contrast to her last writer lover, who spoke ceaselessly about himself, she wondered now that maybe if we were too much in awe of others it kept us from appreciating ourselves. She wondered if Sandro had lost confidence in himself, in the magic of his own talent. When you do that, maybe your Muse flies away, finds someone else to grace.

She had never done that. She never will do that. She had always respected her Self, and that in itself was an homage to whatever god, goddess or lifeforce she sprang from. It was only in loving and honoring ourselves that we could love and honor others. She thought that maybe this is why she always had a healthy capacity to orgasm. She did not take anything for granted, nor did she detest or revile her own flesh.

She left, glad that she would be seeing Leonardo the next night and that she had:

. . . .

RULE #52 If you feel you are not good enough, not worthy, you won't be.

. . . .

CHAPTER 32

NIGHT OF THE LIVING DEAD

She waited now for Leonardo, in the worst (or best) thunderstorm she'd heard in a long time. When it began she thought her upstairs neighbor was moving a large dining table across her ceiling. She was worried though, afraid that he would do what she did and not come. She would be devastated.

She became philosophical in her panic, wondering, *Why is it okay if I am the one to break a date, but not the man? Why does it mean only that I am afraid if I do something like this, but if a man does it, it means he is cruel?*

Maybe intent didn't matter so much, only outcome. She only knew that she felt far too dependent on his arrival. She felt like her self-worth depended on it a little too much. She must relax. She mustn't go to this place. He would only feel it and recoil. But the rain fell so hard, the storm was so strong, she felt swept away. She felt this way all day, like a leaf on the Tiber, insignificant, drifting unnoticed. That afternoon, people at a café sprang to the defense of a wounded pigeon that was being terrorized by a vicious seagull, while among them sat a human girl that felt pecked at by life and its circumstances. She must gather herself, right now, fold herself like a flag into a solid symbol of what she represented: the nation of Artemisia, the country of Self, indivisible, invincible. Her borders were marked, her soldiers on guard. Was this the way she must be?

It finally stopped raining. She waited outside, the smell of jasmine filled the air. Finally she saw his silhouette coming out of the fog. It was 2AM. He was tall, too thin, still so delicious. Her affection for him was real. They spoke briefly, kissed. He was the best Italian kisser she'd known. They had sex—no—they made love. Yet, after a time, it slid down a slope into porn. He grabbed her hair too roughly, pulled her body in such a way that startled and terrified her. She had a spine injury that was quite serious and thought for a moment he'd triggered it. He'd never been this rough before, had he? He also always wanted anal sex…she said no. He didn't argue. While he was always a little rough, he was also always affectionate.

She shared a thought with him that she'd had for a while, "What we have…it's not *l'amore*, but *qualcosa di vicino*"… something that resembled love.

"No," he said, shaking his head. "I am engaged." He pronounced it in three syllables: *en-gah-jed*. He pulled away to the far side of the bed. But her heart was not having it. The old condition pained her. She knew that he cared enough to hold her. She pulled him close, tickled him, made him human again. The next morning, they did it again, had coffee together. But it was all different now. She refused to be upset. She was fine, solid. She took the bus to her office, he left on foot.

"I'll message you," he said.

Maybe, maybe not. But whatever they had now was nowhere near what she thought it was.

She needed her illusions. And damned if they didn't get shattered every time.

. . . .

RULE #53 If someone really loves you, they will try and protect you a little and not shatter *all* your illusions.

. . . .

CHAPTER 33

LONELY, OLD, ASPIE AND UGLY

She was in Trastevere, but she was alone, wandering. The old familiar self-doubt crept in. She was the Witch, the Aspie, the loner. She fought it with all her will. She began to be okay. More than okay. Women looked at her, sometimes she recognized their insecure smiles and she smiled back reassuringly. Sometimes they looked at her with jealousy, occasionally with admiration. Men too stared, and when they judged her, she judged them back: "It is you who is not good enough for me."

She knew what she wanted: she wanted someone who was man enough not to be threatened by the amount of woman that she was. He was nowhere in sight. She wrote, lost herself in thoughts and bruschetta. She headed home…a handsome Frenchman played with his child. She smiled at the boy. The father ushered the child quickly away, lest the witch's mark be upon him. If only he saw how much her own Ama-san loved her, how much people loved her. When you are alone, those with no imagination cannot see how loved you are. They assume no one wants to be with you, just because no one *is* with you.

She thought of her once-beloved Leonardo. She had hoped they could continue a mutual fantasy of sweet innocent affection. But he, for whatever reason, felt compelled to ruin it. She felt nothing for him now beyond what she felt for humanity in general. She was an empty vessel, and this time only the finest wine would fill it.

She dreamt of this man last night. A dark-haired, tattooed love boy that was the same kind of bad boy as her bad girl— honor among devils. Loyalty between partners in crime. Understanding between the misunderstood. Only he 'got' Artemisia. Only with him did she feel completely relaxed and excited at the same time. The only problem was, he did not, to her knowledge, exist.

. . . .

RULE #54 Sometimes we all feel shitty,
ugly, old and alone. It will pass. Do something
fun or nice for yourself in the meantime.

. . . .

. . . .

RULE #55 When you are alone, those with no
imagination cannot see how loved you are.

. . . .

They assume no one wants to be with you, just because no one is with you. You know you are loved, so act like it.

CHAPTER 34

ASPERGIRLS

She met Francesca on the Spanish Steps in a sweltering sun, but the pink-haired pixie was a refreshing sight. Artemisia was able to breathe again in the company of her own kind.

"You are putting yourself on the edge of danger," Francesca told her over lunch. Artemisia had been relating some of her adventures online and Francesca, like many of her friends, had quietly been following.

"If I don't do it who will? I have never had an easy life. I ran away at 14. I was a street kid. I'll never forget coming home from my ice cream job and hearing my stepfather tell my mother I was a little bitch, while my mother said absolutely nothing in my defense." (Her second husband once said that about *her* daughter and she told him if he ever said that again she'd rip his throat out.) "So, I hitch hiked to Florida. I was driven by truckers, taken in by losers, but I never slept with anybody, miraculously. I just stole food and clothes and was some kind of hustler. I still need to know that I can hustle," she added, before conning the waiter into refilling her prosecco for free.

"You are strong, but not all of us can handle it," said Francesca. "We give up, we stop. Life is too hard. Years ago I tried to kill myself, before diagnosis."

"My sister did kill herself. I have wanted to many times. But imagine, how many females have read my books? What kind of message would it send them if I gave up?"

Francesca was a sweet girl. Colorful, petite, a beautiful face that looked just a little sad. She was just now, at 41, finding the courage to be herself. She looked 30 at most. Artemisia relaxed when she was with Asperger women, as long as they were not the angry rigid kind. Those stressed her out. Or the ones who were more borderline than Aspie, with whom you suspected that the ASD diagnosis was given as a palliative measure.

"But also I feel it is my job, my responsibility, to find out what our limits are. If I don't do it, who will? We have only had an identity for the last 25 years but, really, just the last ten. And with my health issues, there is no time to be timid. Women on the spectrum only live to be 57 on average." Donna Williams, a pioneer author on the subject, just died on Artemisia's birthday at age 53, a tragic loss and reminder of this statistic.

In Francesca's presence, Artemisia was reminded of her tribe; she felt her Athenian strength returning. These were her people. They understood her more than any man ever would and certainly more than any neurotypical young man. But, unfortunately, she was a lover of beauty. Maybe this is why she was not bothering to find true love. She didn't believe any man would give her half the understanding and comfort of an AS woman. But they could give her the Adonisian beauty that she craved the way she craved good food, good music, and a soft warm breeze like the one that ruffled the floral ivy surrounding their sidewalk table and played with her hair.

She took the long walk home, exhausted yet renewed.

RULE #56 A woman must be strong and must never give her power away, not to mere boys certainly.

If she was going to play, it would be on her terms. But maybe it was time to find more worthy opponents.

RULE #57 We all need a tribe, to feel like we have a group of people that just innately understand us.

Asperger women were her tribe and probably always would be.

CHAPTER 35

EGO

"Am I a good girl or a vamp?"

"I think you're a good girl. A romantic," responded Kyra, an Aspie friend visiting from Germany.

Artemisia's body recoiled, her spirit railed. "NOOOOO!! It's what people had been saying for decades: You just have to meet the right man, one who deserves you. What if there is no 'right man'? No 'next time'?"

She decided then and there, there was no prince for her. It was the hopeless romantics who fell hardest into despair and cats. She will kill her. She threw a coin into the fountain at Piazza Navona. Rudy the romantic was finally dead. That was her name before. Long live Artemisia. If not long, then happily.

Kyra and Artemisia must be entertained. They liked sex. So, they made plans. They went to the Foro Romano for an afternoon's walk followed by a couple of art showings and then met Sandro and his friend for drinks.

The first art showing was actually a visit to Luigi's studio. She spied his work in a gallery on her last trip to Rome.

So did others, for two days later a large canvas was gone, commanding a high price. It was alive, active, impressive and had that indefinable stroke of genius. He also made an impression on her. She thought of painters as alien creatures. Musicians she could relate to, being one herself and of course with other writers had some kind of kinship, but painters seemed to be made of exotic and mysterious stuff.

"Who are your influences?" she asked him.

"Myself," he responded.

Good answer. When she was writing something, she could not read other people. And she was almost always writing something. She read before she was published, enough books to fill a small library. Now she could not risk the voices of others crowding out her own.

Kyra and she went to an art gallery for an opening...the art seemed flaccid compared to Luigi's. They left quickly and went to a snob café. Women dared to stare with judgment but she stared back as if to say "I am the Queen and you should not be so bold." She liked Artemisia. This woman was in control.

They met Sandro and his friend at Piazza Trilussa. The friend had so much cologne on she could not stay near. Sandro was still handsome. They went in search of drinks.

On the way they passed Jermaine, a street artist and merchant she befriended, who spoke seven languages fluently. He was also—with his dreadlocks pointing up—about seven feet tall. He looked at unwitting Sandro as if he wanted to rip his head off. She smiled secretly, this newly-born bad girl. *At least someone is into me.* Not, unfortunately, her type. He was too aggressive.

Sandro led them to her mecca, Ego Café, where she'd met Luigi, Damiano, and where she had recently flirted with Faustus. The latter was there, behind the bar, fuming. She knew it was petty but she still liked the fact that men were jealous over her, almost for the first time in her life.

Sandro and she had what she thought was a great conversation. She tried not to talk about herself too much, and she made sure to praise him, his mind, his advice. His friend was very nice too, once the cologne settled down and took a back seat. They talked about writing, life, love. Kyra was quieter than her, as usual. She was a Brazilian goddess and didn't need to do much. Artemisia always talked too much when she was in the mood to socialize.

"That picture is corny," said Sandro, looking at one of her album covers, "but I'm a nerd," was his reasoning.

She had not thought of him as such. With his black curls, long, still-lithe body, and cherubic face, he looked not unlike Michelangelo's David. He seemed more beautiful and interesting to her tonight than the other. She sensed that while he was not repelled, he was also not *that* into her and she didn't know why exactly. She would leave and let him think about it.

"It's time for me and Kyra to go, sorry."

Both the men protested, although it may have been his friend first. But Sandro did say, "Come with us."

She decided that if he texted her after they parted, she would meet them later. He gave her the coldest of air kisses, near each cheek in the Italian style.

"Don't you want to kiss me?" she asked him.

"No," he said, backing away. "This is not the time or the place."

What was? she wondered. The women left, and she told Kyra everything that had happened. Kyra had been deep in conversation with the friend.

"Maybe you talked too much. Men like a mystery. You can't make them think you are better than them. Not until after they fall in love with you."

She thought back over the conversation. Was she dominating? She didn't feel like it, she felt like it was even, well-matched. Back and forth. Millions of years of evolution and she's supposed to go back to the trees? Why didn't she just take his laundry down to the Tiber and pound it on a rock?

Did she deflate his drive because she had the audacity to speak about her new manuscript a little? She didn't speak of any of her old ones and changed the subject when asked about her life. She was so tired of fragile male egos...did she stroke his ego too hard or not hard enough? Do they think to themselves: *Did I stroke her ego too hard or not hard enough?* No. They just do what they do and we have to adapt around them like water around a rock. She's tired of having to think so hard. She liked kissing, holding, fucking, so she didn't have to think. But Sandro refused to kiss her.

Kyra had been single for a month. She had five or six lovers all lined up and waiting for her. Artemisia had been single for six months and she had no lovers at the moment. She thought of her little American boy. Slim, effeminate, a tiger in bed. What made him *not* afraid of her? What set him apart? American confidence?

Maybe, on some molecular level, she was looking for a Chopin to her George Sand. And they sensed it. When they felt they were not worthy, they turned it around and blamed it on her being a witch, on the things that she said. Or maybe she was just an ass.

The women stopped in to a bar. She needed an espresso before climbing the hill to bed. She was too perplexed now to stay out.

"Where you from? You are beautiful…isn't she beautiful?" asked a very drunk customer, before knocking a glass to the floor. Whatever was inside splashed Artemisia from shoulder to toe.

The barista he was talking to was already mopping the floor. He joked with the drunk about licking it off of her but then reverted to, "Yes, she's beautiful," when he saw the look on Artemisia's face.

She left, disheartened and tired.

At home, she went online and found pictures of Sandro at several media events, signing books, flanked by women in bikinis. He was a golden boy, just like Rasputin. Somewhere in there, she guessed, he fell in love. He had mentioned it and his face went dark. He had lost his rhythm, his confidence long before Artemisia. It wasn't her. Nevertheless, she was tired of taking only knowledge to bed with her.

Weeks later, she messaged him and asked him if she'd done something, something to offend him.

"You couldn't be more wrong," he responded. Nevertheless, they never met again.

. . . .

RULE #58 Everyone has a past. And you don't know how much of it is affecting their present.

. . . .

Months later, she sat up in bed with a sudden realization: Roman men liked to kiss with tongues from the onset and, in that case, it was definitely true that Ego Cafe with the two dozen people watching, would not have been the time and place. She rolled over and fell back asleep, smiling to herself: "Sometimes, Artemisia, you are an overanalyzing dumbass."

CHAPTER 36

A CHERUB IN FIRENZE

Kyra and Artemisia took a train to Firenze. They wanted to explore other cities, imagine life in another place, another time. Upon arrival they immediately sensed that it was very different to Rome. Not a single man smiled at them or said 'hello,' instead they pushed past with their perfectly-sculpted hair, eyes straight ahead, lest they reveal anything about themselves. Oh, the women found that so boring. They meandered through narrow streets, avoiding tourist crowds as best they could and headed vaguely towards the river and the Uffizi Gallery. They had little time and literally no plans.

On the way, they stumbled across the large 1910 copy of Michelangelo's 'David' set in the Piazza della Signoria. The original was kept away from the elements in the Accademia Gallery.

"Must be nice to have a clone," Artemisia joked.

She would love to be able to stay home in bed reading every night, while a copy of her went out and had all these potentially debilitating adventures. Nearby, was 'Perseus clutching the head of Medusa' and many other renaissance marvels, still perfectly preserved. A little while later they came across a statue of Dante Alighieri, a figure in Kyra's life for many years. She'd met her husband at a school called by that very name. And now, years later, the couple were parting. Artemisia waited behind so Kyra could visit the statue alone. This was private.

A few minutes later, in a shop, they heard a favorite song from Kyra's youth.

"The gods and goddesses don't so much as whisper to me here in Florence, but they are shouting at you," Artemisia told her. "You are doing the right thing."

Kyra just smiled seductively in agreement. She'd blossomed from a wallflower to a trailing ivy, wandering and decorating everything that she touched. She spoke, people listened, she smiled, and they fell in love. Sometimes the best way to live was for something to die.

They sat in a café in the Piazza della Republica, when Artemisia spied a bald man with a motorcycle helmet and high heels walking with a young lad, a dark cherub. They sat on a stone bench, the young one's feet not even touching the stones below. His head was turned up coquettishly toward the older man. He talked the whole while, swinging one of his legs like a girl in a 1930s musical. He had a perfect Botticelli cherub face, except that his skin was dark, not fair, his hair black, not golden as they were always depicted, but he had the perfect cupid's bow mouth. The older man was captivated. Artemisia was not one to judge; age and knowledge made that too heavy of a burden, but she hoped fervently that this was not a young teen as he looked but a very clever hustler who played up his youthful air.

. . . .

RULE #59 Children are sacred.

. . . .

Until such time as they chose to cross the line into adulthood and were *capable* of such a choice they must be spared adults' dark and depraved ways. This applied to men and women alike; she'd met a man the other night who told her that he was raped by a woman when he was 17 and it affected him his whole life. While they didn't delve into *how* it affected him, she could still see the child in his eyes, wondering *why*. As humans, it was our responsibility to care for each other.

The women left the dark energy of Firenze and took the fast train home. For Rome was, for the moment, home. They got off the train with renewed energy and practically floated back to Trastevere. Smiles, *ciaos*, *buonaseras* from some of the world's most outgoing men serenaded them along the way. She saw Sandro with a blonde woman. Of course he was. He no longer seemed to shine with a special light. Maybe, as Rasputin once said, she did shine a light. Maybe this was why men shone when they were with her—they were reflecting hers. Artemisia saw their beauty in her light, but perhaps they just felt exposed.

Nevermind him. She determined to get herself a kiss. She walked through the busiest street looking for her winner. All of a sudden, a gorgeous face with fair skin, black hair, slanted eyes and pursed lips appeared out of the crowd, making kissing noises in an exaggerated manner…*"mwah!"* it said. She *"mwah'd"* back. She was satisfied that for now,

. . . .

RULE #60 The chase, and the chaste,
might be more fun than the having.

. . . .

CHAPTER 37

DUE UOMINI

Kyra heard Artemisia talking Italian in her sleep. She may not be speaking it consciously but subconsciously she was singing it like a siren. Today was a laid back day. They visited Vatican City, or, as Kyra liked to call it, "Catholic Disneyland."

There may be many treasures of art inside the buildings, but Artemisia was not one to stand in line like cattle, in the bright sun for three hours. Kyra bought some plastic overpriced wares from a gift shop and that was it.

Afterward, they returned to Trastevere and waited for the hormonals to wake up and return. Meanwhile, it was Aperol Spritz, pasta and cappuccinos at various outdoor restaurants. A young waiter she remembered from her last time there was reeled in.

"What time are you working 'til?"

"Eleven," he said. "Come and get me."

He looked like a much younger and handsomer version of Tom Cruise. The women left, heading for the stairs of Piazza Trilussa, a popular meeting place.

Artemisia announced, "I'm getting a kiss."

Before they walked 20 metres, a young Persian man popped out of a doorway, pleading for her to have a drink with him. He was emphatic. Another Aperol Spritz, shared. Hamid didn't speak very much English, other than the word "hotel." Artemisia got her kiss from Hamid, while his older friend, a colleague, spoke awkwardly with Kyra.

There was nothing menacing about Hamid. He was handsome, virile, sexy, polite, passionate and he wanted Artemisia, full stop. For some reason, this thing which would have been unfathomable to her at any other time of her life, was not offensive, it was hot. She was extremely turned on. The pheromones of Rome made her feel 14 again, except without the Christian American guilt.

"Do you mind waiting?" she asked Kyra.

"No. How long will you be gone?"

"Cinque minuti," she told her. Five minutes. Hamid seemed fit to burst. They walked away from the bustling street they were on and again, she followed her nose. She found a dark corner against a stone wall of a parking area.

There was graffiti on the wall that said *"It is the role of the artist to make revolution irresistible."*

"How old are you?" he had asked her as they walked.

"Trenta-tre," she told him. Thirty-three.

It was for his benefit. Otherwise, he would be too distracted. What difference did it make? She didn't want to marry him.

"You are 23," she told him. His friend had told Kyra.

"No, I'm 26."

So the young want to be older and the old want to be young. Be where you are. And right now, she was fucking Hamid against the stone wall of a Roman parking lot. It was a fantasy come true. So what if he was a wine salesman and not a gladiator? He was fit enough to be one.

Afterwards, they returned to their friends, and she and Hamid parted company. She and Kyra and her messy hair got a couple of beers and headed to Piazza Trilussa, finally. There was a reggae duo playing, singer/guitarist, and a percussionist. The women didn't normally like reggae but tonight it was splendid. An African danced and sent rainbows of good energy into the crowd. Artemisia spied a handsome man, two of them, talking together. Kyra and she took a turn around the square like Victorian ladies, then went back to their spot at the top of the stairs. She felt like a queen surveying her kingdom. The men seemed to leave for a bit, but then were back. He was staring at Artemisia, the one that first caught her eye. Suddenly they appeared on the steps next to the women. He was speaking rapidly in Italian.

"No parlo Italiano," she told him.

His friend translated roughly. "He is a doctor, his heart is going 'boom boom' for you."

At first she fell for it but after a time it was evident he was no doctor, he was just a bad boy, like most men she was attracted to. He wanted to be alone with her. At first she said yes, but she had a moment or two of doubt, when she found out she had to get in a car with them.

"Let's go," said Kyra with a naughty but supportive smile. "It's okay."

They went to his house, drove farther than she was comfortable with. Kyra and the friend waited outside in the tiny garden smoking cigarettes.

"Trenta minuti," Artemisia told her. "Order a taxi."

She didn't get to finish with Hamid earlier. Being a little worried they might be caught made him cum fast, but just left her walking funny. Women do get hardons, they're just internal so they can't be seen. She was determined to orgasm this time. This man liked cunnilingus, so much that she almost had to order him to stop and fuck her. It was hot—so hot—partly because she knew that Kyra and the friend were probably hearing at least some of it.

When she exited the bedroom, she was fairly stunned to find them sitting just outside the bedroom door in the living room.

"Oh my god, I'm so embarrassed. If I had known you were right outside the door I wouldn't have said what I said." Her usual—*cum on my tits, fuck me baby, etc.* The kind of crap learned from porn that always seemed to work.

"We didn't hear anything," Kyra smiled. "Just some banging."

Kyra was not only happy for her friend, but kind of got a little inspired and used the time wisely. On the way home in the car, Artemisia watched her toy with the other man in the visor mirror. She heard him say "no touch, no touch," and wondered what that was about. Later Kyra told her that she enjoyed playing him, the erotic teasing of it all, and that is what she had said to him when they were on the couch. She had a few suitors now and didn't want more.

Meanwhile Artemisia's lover revealed his true ignorant nature. Now that he'd had his way with her, he felt free to yell about the drink she'd brought in the car, where they needed to be dropped off, and anything else that crossed his pea brain. When they finally were let out of his car, she practically jumped out. Of all the men she'd met on this adventure, he was one of the ones she really didn't like. She'd already forgotten his name.

Back at home Kyra said, "Poor boy, he was probably waiting for us."

"Handsome waiter boy! We forgot all about him." She thought that he may have been a better investment of her time. But regrets were not something she ever engaged in.

She remembered one of her earlier rules, that men would make up things about themselves to get a woman in bed. Now she vowed to listen to her instincts; if she were feeling any doubt, to honor *that* and not some stranger's needs and urges…or even the good-natured support of a friend.

"He was handsome. I wonder if he knows it," Artemisia said, referring to the Tom Cruise look-alike.

"I don't think he does," Kyra replied.

"Ooh, a real prince."

"Princes are for princesses," said her trusty friend. "We are no princesses. We want bad boys."

The next morning, Kyra caught a taxi to the airport and returned home. Artemisia missed her already. Still, the one feeling she was left with was not guilt, or regret, but she simply didn't like the second man. And it was dangerous to get in the car with strangers. This, she would not do again.

RULE #61 Listen to your instincts and go with your gut. If you have hesitation, hesitate. When in doubt, leave it out.

And,

RULE #62 Don't let prejudice, whether religious or political, prevent you from seeing and experiencing the beauty of people from other cultures.

Hamid was born in a Muslim country. She had never been with one before, religious or not. (Hamid wasn't, she'd asked.) We were *all* told, in a million different ways, to believe that people with our own skin color, religion, flag etc. are superior (Americans more than most). People are people and there are no good people and no bad people. Only good acts and bad acts.

CHAPTER 38

CONDOMS

"You are mine this night!" said the message.

She had thought they were over, but apparently, going into his café when he wasn't there, and ignoring him completely when she walked by, worked like a charm on Leonardo. The day after Kyra left, he messaged her.

He was so skinny that Artemisia felt concerned that he might be sick, that it might even be HIV. He took a test he bought from a drug store and sent her a photo of the result. Negative. She and Leonardo had never used condoms. She'd thought he was too innocent to worry. Now she ran out and bought her own test. A few nerve-wracking minutes later, came the result. Negative.

Leonardo slept over and for the first time, he held her tightly most of the night. This was their fourth date. While the second and third ended with her feeling a bit shitty, this time things were going well. Very little talk of his girlfriend and much mention of going to see Artemisia in France or wherever she would be. This was how to play it. She didn't want him to love her, and he didn't disrespect her, because she didn't disrespect herself. She was doing what she wanted, because it felt good, and it was fun. She even told him about the two men the day before.

He, in turn, told her about all the women he'd been with, and how with some he'd engaged in anal sex. She'd thought that it was rare, but apparently not. They'd done it together, her and Leonardo. When she was younger, she had a phase where she not only loved it, she almost required it. It became addictive, like a lot of things that feel good. And it could feel good if you relaxed and knew what you were doing. But it was high risk behavior. There was almost a guarantee of a tiny bit of skin breakage, tearing and of course, body fluid exchange. In fact, many men liked anal sex precisely because they could cum into a woman without getting her pregnant. They could, however, give her HIV or a dozen other diseases.

"With condoms?" she asked.

Of course he said 'yes' but she no longer believed him. In fact, it had only been lately that she herself had begun to be consistently safe. Once more they made love, for that is what it felt like, only this time, she was armed with knowledge and latex. About 5AM, just as she was dozing off, Leonardo's phone rang. His mum or his girlfriend. Could be either, with these Roman boys. She didn't look, she wasn't that kind.

"How many times did my phone ring in the night?" he asked in the morning.

"It buzzed once or twice."

He left after coffee looking a little sad. "Good*bye*, Artemisia," he said somewhat dramatically.

She liked to think it was because she was leaving Rome the next day, but more likely it was because he was feeling guilty. He had a sweet, beautiful girlfriend waiting for him somewhere. And, in her heart, she will know. Women always do.

The number 22 had always meant something to Artemisia. It was the date of her birthday. It was the age Jonathan (a man she'd always considered to be the love of her life) was when she met him. It was two of her anniversaries, with Rasputin and one of her weddings. It was in two of her book titles. It was Leonardo's age; the threshold between youth and old age, where a young man is still enthusiastic, not jaded, eager to learn. Before they settled down with a woman, or began a cycle of brief if not failed relationships. They were at the height of their physical prowess at the same moment. Such a moment.

To fill in the gaps between meeting men IRL (in real life), at Kyra's suggestion she joined a dating site called Tinder. Every man had the same photos—cars, bikes, motorcycles, jumping out of planes—like they all wanted to be James Bond. Meanwhile she knew that they mostly all had mundane jobs and sat around in their underpants watching football, not playing it. She would never choose a 22-year-old on Tinder. But, in life, they chose each other.

She went shopping and then to a café. Classic bad boy waiter…mmm he was exactly what she liked—black hair, tattoos. For some reason he sneered at her. Let him. It didn't bother her in the slightest. There were always going to be those who thought they were too cool for her, but she couldn't waste her time worrying about them. The trouble with Aspergirls was they let people like this get to them. Not Artemisia, not anymore. She played with the Australian across the way. She played with the Italian trio next to her. She play play played. She made eyes at the chaste husband and watched him stare back hungrily. Rasputin would have been proud.

She would give anything to be in a committed relationship again. But he had broken her faith and trust so badly, she was no longer sure it was possible. Until then,

· · · · · · · · · · · · · · · · · · · ·

RULE #7 *again*. Condoms, tests and more condoms!

· · · · · · · · · · · · · · · · · · · ·

Short of total fidelity there would be no other way to survive this new life.

CHAPTER 39

MICHELANGELO AND MONA LISA

The night was young and she needed food. She went to see Orlando the pizza boy, literally one of the most beautiful young men she had ever seen in her life. Kyra liked him, so she went to tell him so. He stalled Artemisia's order, took several customers before her so they could talk. His English was perfect. His brother played football for England and he lived with him there. She knew nothing about football. But she did know beauty and this one had it in spades. He was also nice, kind, he was always friendly and he wasn't afraid of her. Or Kyra, for she remembered to show him her picture.

"We will hang out," he said.

"She's left already."

"No, I mean me and you."

She bounced back to her tram, pizza, beer and clothes shopping dangling awkwardly in her hand. But she didn't drop it. "I got this."

She knew now why the Mona Lisa smirked…

He was late. Handsome pizza boy. She had to get up early for a flight, but he promised sushi and red wine and implied much more. When she got home the night before, he had messaged her. She ignored it, but in the morning she casually responded. Next thing she knew, they embarked on a day-long flirt. Going through his photos she discovered one that was very possibly the most beautiful photograph of a man she had ever seen. Usually, no matter how good looking, they have some quirk that made them less than perfect. Either they looked a bit silly, or terribly vain, or had chipmunk cheeks, or something. This man, perfect. She stared at his washboard, six-pack stomach so long that it began to be a perseveration. A drug. She realized that she had to have him or she would physically pine for him and feel as if she had missed out on something truly special.

She didn't kid herself he was intelligent. It became clear pretty quickly that he was no scholar, genius or artist. But he might be an artist of a sort...in bed. She wanted to find out.

All day she looked forward to it, hungered for him, red wine and sushi. She wasn't sure if red wine and sushi would even go together but she was willing to bet it would be delicious this time.

Then, he dropped the mini-bomb. "I'm just going to take a nap," he said. Their appointed rendezvous time rolled round and passed...her intuition told her he was coming though, so she didn't despair or even feel pissed off like the old (young) her would have.

When Orlando was late for their date she decided "don't get mad, get shots" and popped into Mr Brown's, a tiny dive in Trastevere famous for their 'porno shots.' Delicious vodka, chocolate and cayenne concoctions that went down like kids' play but could result in some very adult behavior.

She grabbed the first two handsome men she saw and asked, "Can you please let me take my picture with you? My date is late and I want him to see that I'm not sitting around waiting...alone." One of them had the nicest shine about him. Black hair, glasses, trendy mini-beard, and a guitar case. Musicians. She never took them seriously in the lover department. She knew how self-centred they were. He asked for her name and she gave him her card.

It was after midnight when Orlando finally arrived. He was so tall that she was not sure they were even on a date. In fact, she felt like she was on a date with Britney Spears, for that was the t-shirt he wore. When she was younger she would have rather eaten sand than gone on a date with anyone mainstream enough to wear a BS shirt without irony. But things like that didn't matter quite as much now on... whatever this was. A booty date—a beauty date. Orlando looked over her head the whole time. But she didn't let his cavalier attitude deter her, not even when she caught him checking out a polyester blonde. She didn't let his height, his beauty or his age intimidate her. She got in his face as much as she could, being a foot shorter.

It wasn't long before they just decided to go to her place. This was not a deep story, but yet, it was.

Looking at him in the glow of a single candle, she said what was in her heart: "You are the reason that Michelangelo carved men out of stone."

His was the most perfect beauty imaginable. Thick black curls, perfect features head to toe. She couldn't even say that his beauty had no character, because it did. She made him kiss her over and over, deeply and sensuously, despite his tendency at first to act like he was in a porn film. He was wonderful, strong, almost violent and then tender—the way she liked it. She could have used a bit more tender but they were not making love, they were fucking. This was *una bella scopata*.

He was sweet like a puppy, preoccupied with his hair like a teenage girl, talked about his mum like a good Italian boy. But he fucked and looked like a Roman god. They talked about their favorite Roman sites, and his was the Coliseo, of course. She could picture him there, years ago, whether as an emperor or pauper, a soldier or a senator. He belonged in that landscape and that landscape belonged to men like him.

"How old are you?" He asked her.

"What difference does it make? This is not love, I am not meeting your mama."

"I want to know."

"How old do you think I am?" she asked.

"Thirty."

"OK, I'm 30."

He left at 3AM. She passed out from exhaustion, and woke feeling like she gave Rita a belated birthday present. That was her name when she was young. Rita always loved beautiful boys, but they didn't love her. Tab Bowman was 17 and she was 12 and she wanted him. She wasn't sure what sex was but she knew she wanted it with him. He hit her in the leg with a shovel and said,

"You're not a girl, I don't know *what* you are."

That was a million years ago. Orlando was only six years older than Tab was then. It took her that long to learn how to talk to men, to boys, so that she wouldn't scare them. She could still scare them if she wanted, but she didn't want. It was so easy, there was almost no point to it.

. . . .

RULE #63 Maybe some people aren't that intellectual, but so what? There are different reasons to feel affection for someone.

. . . .

Neither are dogs and we love them, don't we? And, just like animals sense when someone doesn't like them, so do people. Maybe that's why that demographic and hers traditionally did not mesh. They sensed our contempt and returned it twofold. Or vice versa. Each situation would be different of course. But neurotypical (NT) men like this could be affectionate, sweet, sometimes they could be brilliant. She got what she wanted, after all those years. She made love to a god, a dog, a mortal and a man. And she was smirking like the Mona Lisa.

CHAPTER 40

PRESSING CHARGES

She booked an apartment in Paris in the Butte aux Cailles, a neighborhood she knew well. The train from the airport took her to the Metro 7 which dropped her right outside his door. She could have landed elsewhere, but she was craving the foods and sights and smells of yore. She wanted her favorite Vietnamese Pho and some of the best pastry in Paris. And of course, she wanted to see if she would run into *him*.

As she stumbled though the district, exhausted from some crazy weeks in Rome, she passed bars buzzing with young people, mostly men. She got looks. She never used to get looks when she lived here. Mostly because Rasputin would be out at parties, or on dates with women, while she spent evenings alone and waited for him to return to her. Wandering the streets by herself most evenings she felt lonely, unloved, stupid. Usually he would return around 2:30AM or so and she'd listen to him talk about himself till dawn. Then they'd have sex. Great sex. She loved him once. Deeply. She checked herself for the old feelings. They were gone. Dead. She was still reminiscing and smiling about the beauty and sweetness of Hamid and Orlando. Fuck *Le Douchebag*. This is what he wanted: an independent Artemisia that didn't need him. The tradeoff was that she no longer wanted him. That, she thought, is what made him so angry he had to ruin her reputation.

She passed out early and woke at dawn, not wanting to be there. She rose slowly, got a latte across the street which, in typical French contrariness, turned out to be a cappuccino. A delicious one. The waiter rather bitchily brought it to her. *"Tu peux sourire,"* she told him. You can smile. "It's free."

He looked at her funny for a moment and cracked a small one. Next thing she knew, she heard humming and singing…there were some good tunes playing and he sang right along. She caught him checking her out a few times. He was exactly the kind she used to fall for, a young Richard Chamberlain mixed with Richard Butler. She wrestled with her tablet, which decided that the camera would no longer work for some reason, then looked up to see three extremely gorgeous young men crossing the intersection at various angles. They would have all seemed unapproachable to her last year, because none were smiling. Being a literal Aspie, a smile and a compliment said you were interested. A scowl said you were not. That was the difference between Rome and Paris. Here you were uncool if you showed your joy. If she could wave a wand, she'd make that go away. But that was also the difference between her now and then. She was no longer intimidated. Athena had waved her wand over her.

Artemisia came here to press charges against the man that beat her up last year and then set out on a behind-the-scenes smear campaign, even affecting her book sales in France. She realized at this moment that, if she did press charges, he would merely revel in the attention. It would only add to his illusion that he was important. She remembered how the two of them watched those women on TV talking about how Bill Cosby, a famous comedian, allegedly drugged and raped them. They were earnest and tearful and no one with half a brain really doubted them.

"I would never do that," she told Rasputin, "play the victim. They look weak and stupid, even though what he did was terribly wrong. I'd handle it differently."

The waiter handed her the change with a smile and a deep look and said, "bonne journée."

Frenchmen could be so lovely, she thought. *It will be a good day.*

CHAPTER 41

JUNE, NOT APRIL, IN PARIS

Paris was not a great place to be a single lady with no girlfriends. Leticia was the only one she had left after all her time there and she wasn't even French, she was Ukrainian. Artemisia loved her girlfriends around the world, whether Italian, Greek, Aussie, American, German, Brazilian, etc. and wished she could have them all in one place. She cried when Leticia left their lunch date. She usually only did that when she was not going to see someone again or if she knew they would be very changed, like a small child who would be a foot taller when you saw them again and you will have missed everything in between.

Leticia had been holding onto her guitar for her. Artemisia returned to her room and played, with fingers quickly blistering from a month of disuse. She embraced the instrument, overwhelmed with emotion. She realized at that moment, that she came to Paris to be reunited with her true love—her guitar. Her music.

Afterward, she attempted a glass of wine at the same café. She wanted a ciggie so she asked a waiter for one. She did this in Rome all the time. Even if they didn't smoke, they'd find you one.

"I only have enough for myself," he sneered.

She didn't get even a glass of water with her wine. She reminisced about Roman *aperitivo*—an entire buffet that comes almost free with one drink. When she finished, she had to get cash from an ATM as they didn't take cards. He took her bag so she wouldn't run away. A Roman man would simply watch you with his dark eyes, hoping you would run so he could chase you. She began to hate Paris.

She slept. She walked a little, trying to find the beauty she once believed was there. She felt weak, exhausted. It was obvious she was becoming ill again. But it didn't seem to have a specific cause.

She wrote to Kyra, "Can I come and stay with you for a while? I hate to sound like Jane Eyre but I'm having a bit of a collapse."

Fortunately Kyra said yes. On the last day Artemisia took a bus to Gare de l'Est, happy to be leaving. Too many cars, too noisy, too many people not smiling. Take away the cars and you'd have something. But the air was so bad she felt starved of oxygen.

She got off the bus at the station and then it hit her: the smell. It was cooler just for a moment and the result was that it smelled like April in Paris. Ella Fitzgerald began to sing in her head so loudly she couldn't hear anything else. It was just like last Spring when she returned to him. After their three month long first date, after he cheated on her and she slapped him. After he threw her across the room. After the bruises. After the long flight back alone. After the aching weeks, she went back to him. It was a beautiful reunion. Even though he cheated on her again, she convinced herself he was only trying to prove a point. Then it was just her and him. They stayed up all night on that last night, having dinner, holding hands, promising eternal love, if not fidelity.

"We will always be lovers," he said. "I will never ignore you again."

It was April in Paris. They slow danced to that very song, made love on the floor where she'd lain broken.

"Hurry back," he'd said.

And she did. She knew now that she should have left it at that, brought her things home with her instead of leaving them in his house. Never gone back, except maybe once in a while, to see the Seine and be with him.

But she was not yet Artemisia. She was Rudy, the innocent. The one that believed in true love, in one man for one woman. It wasn't until their last week, the night before their one year anniversary, that she began to die. She finally went to see him perform his play. It was her night. She had coached him, healed him, made him a better man and, therefore, a better actor. But he went home with another woman. Artemisia waited for him at his house, in his bed, while a storm raged outside, a storm more ferocious than any she'd ever experienced in Paris.

She left for Athens, just for a few days. "Hurry back," he said. She never saw him again.

Artemisia sat in the train station feeling very strongly that things could have gone very differently if she had known what he was, what she was. The smell of piss suddenly filled her nostrils—from where? It was so strong she couldn't even tell. The homeless people, the ancient plumbing, the bad food? She didn't know. But it was not April in Paris, it was June and, as the pavement heated up, the stew of blood, piss, vomit, cigarettes, fuel, spilled beer, shit and everything else created a fume that was as repugnant to her as he was now.

Artemisia waited for her train…and couldn't wait to get back to her new life, wherever that may be. Never again to be fooled by a man. But, first, to her friend, to the love and safety of Kyra…

CHAPTER 42

BITTER BLOOD MOON

"The blood is the life." "Take my blood and drink it." We see it everywhere. In films, religion, games and war... Blood, blood, blood. Most of the men she had been with did not mind a bit of blood during sex. In fact, sex often stimulated the onset of a period if it was reluctant to start. But no one talked about it. Even on popular porn sites, where you could find almost anything, there wasn't one category for blood, periods, menstruation, nothing.

Artemisia met Zafeer at a Brazilian music party at an outdoor café in Frankfurt. He was with a group of friends, including many women, but couldn't stop staring at her. She went inside and down the stairs to the bathroom. He followed. They chatted, and then spoke outside alone for a while. He was a PhD student. She saw the photos of the lecture halls, the conferences, it would had to have been an elaborate ruse, assembled within the first few minutes of meeting her, if he were not. He had the innocent professor vibe, but she loved intelligent men. They were usually much more nuanced lovers, even if they were competitive with her.

His friend came and retrieved him after only about ten minutes, "We have to leave now." The man gave Artemisia what she could only describe as a dirty look. She wondered why.

"When are you going back to Rome?" Zafeer asked.

"Tomorrow."

She'd been at Kyra's for ten days, mostly sleeping and making silly music videos with her friend. She was now strong enough to leave.

When Zafeer left with his group about a half hour later, she blew him a kiss.

In the morning, a message: "I want to see you."

"Then you'll have to come to Rome," she replied.

"What flight are you on?"

After several messages, she and Kyra picked him up from the train station. He was coming with her.

It was clear from the first moment there was something. But she was not prepared for what happened when he kissed her at the station. She swooned like she was in an old Hollywood film. All the way to the airport he massaged her shoulders from the backseat, played with her hands from behind. He had a sexy yet gentle, kind nature and she was glowing in a way she had not done in a long time.

"I never did this," he said, "follow a woman to another country."

She wanted to say it was the first time a man followed her. It wasn't, but he was her first Kurd.

By the time they got to her apartment in Rome they were both fit to burst. The way he kissed her in the station was nothing compared to being in bed with him. He was only her second Muslim, and like Hamid—not religious, but he was mystical. He had told her that he spent his youth hiding in mountain villages among mystics who could levitate for 15 seconds, he'd counted. He himself had put a large iron nail through his cheeks with no pain and no blood. There was something otherworldly in his sexual prowess. She'd rarely encountered anything like it. When she came it felt like they were engulfed in a beautiful light.

Only her blood brought them back down to earth. Her period, which had been hanging on and on, but was just about at its end, returned in full force from the flight. That often happened when she flew, probably the change in cabin pressure. He had been using a condom but it was consumed by the blood, by the process of sex and by his ejaculation. It had practically disappeared inside her. The fact that he touched her blood frightened him. She explained that she'd just taken an HIV test, that she had no communicable diseases that she knew of and that since the test, she'd been diligently practicing safe sex. They did it again in the shower. He kept stopping to wash the blood off of him. But the experience of being with him was still exquisite.

"How long can you keep doing this, Artemisia?"

She knew exactly what he meant. Sleeping around, living in apartments which were not hers. Eating in restaurants, being away from family. Not belonging anywhere.

"As long as I need to."

She didn't tell him that she needed to exorcize the demon of Rasputin from her soul, what was left of it. That since she didn't belong to him she felt like she didn't belong anywhere. She wanted to belong somewhere, to someone. Who doesn't? She slept beautifully in Zafeer's arms.

The next morning was perfect. He made her delicious coffee which he served her in bed. They went for an early lunch of pasta to fortify them for a long stroll to the *Foro Romano*, a place she knew he must see. They kissed passionately in the *Palatino*, the site of ancient Rome spread out beneath them, oblivious to the families and children all around. They were in Rome, they must expect to see such things. Zafeer titillated and tantalized her with his words and with his sexy touch.

As they walked home he asked her, "Are you mildly autistic, or more than mildly?"

"What do you think?" she asked.

"More than," he said.

Maybe it was the way she bumped her head on the glass as she tried to look out of the window that morning (twice), or perhaps her complete lack of sense of direction. Maybe it was her incurable innocence, despite her rampant sexual thirst. She laughed and they held hands all the way across Circo Massimo.

Never throw a hat upon a bed, for all your good dreams will turn up dead. She knew this. She was not terribly superstitious, but she'd seen it before—bad things would always happen immediately after. It was bad luck. She did it this morning by mistake.

After their outing they decided to go to Zafeer's hotel room which he had not yet even seen. They began to make love, and there was a tiny bit of blood. Clearly her period was on its way out. He came rather quickly, pulled out and ran off to the shower to wash. He was gone five minutes but it might as well have been five hours. She had an immediate, internal but violent reaction to him ripping himself from her arms. He helped to bring her to climax after he came back a few minutes later but she still hadn't recovered from his abrupt departure. She felt upset, annoyed, almost angry. She even wanted to cry.

"It felt violent when you ran off to the bathroom after your needs were met. I wasn't done. I still needed to be held. I don't need to feel diseased just because of a bit of blood!"

Zafeer argued rather than apologized. He clearly had an aversion to blood beyond the rational. It was too neurotic for her.

"I want to leave now." She wanted to go alone. But his stuff was at her place.

She thought about other men, less complicated men, but then she stopped and remembered how Leonardo made her cry, how Romero annoyed her, or this one did that or that one did this, and she realized there was no sex without complications for her. Not usually. For she fell in love. Every time…for a little while. Sometimes for minutes, hours, a day or two. And then she fell out of love. The only ones that she stayed in love with were the ones that sort of kept her on a tense string. She realized fully how messed-up that was. She feared that she would never be able to have a healthy relationship.

As they walked back to hers in the late afternoon sun they stopped for gelato. The cold and sugar helped, but only a little. Zafeer was quiet, meek, sad. Such a sensitive young man. Could this be the same person who made her cum so fiercely the night before, and who had filled her with desire all day with his open-minded talk about sex? She'd hurt him. He kept wanting to kiss her. She no longer wanted to, full stop.

"I needed this dose of reality," she told him. "I was getting too starry-eyed."

It was true. She put men, including him, on a pedestal the moment she had sex with them, especially if they popped her rockets the way he did. He understood her, understood her needs perhaps better than most. He even implied he wanted to help her, but she didn't see how he could. The only help she needed was financial and it was slowly becoming clear… he was broke. He'd fallen off the pedestal.

"When you are on the autism spectrum, you are perpetually naive. We are always looking for the Disney version of love and when that *fable bubble* is burst, we react like children."

She realized at this moment that she did not have the capacity to love someone. Not romantically. Not in a healthy reciprocal way. She had never realized this before. Okay, then she was free. Free to feel affection, camaraderie, for many people. Although she'd thought she was a 'one man woman,' she was really just a 'one myth woman.' And that myth, like almost all of the ones she'd been told, was now destroyed, cast aside like so many other childhood fairy tales.

He brought his moroseness into her apartment yet expected to stay the night with her. She now really wanted him to leave.

"I went into the red for you!" Zafeer was shouting now.

"You overdrew your bank account? That is not my problem!"

He finally left. They did not sleep together again.

She saw him again the next evening, his last in Rome. They sat by the Tiber quietly. He was deeply sad. "I feel as if I am in some kind of movie," he said. *"Bitter Moon."*

He was not the first to equate her with the character of Mimi. But Artemisia was not out for retribution. She was not going back to push her old lover around in any wheelchair, real or metaphorical. She was living and loving life. And looking forward.

"I am glad we met, Zafeer."

The experience with him changed her. She wept several times over the next days, for the tender soul she hurt, for the lost soul trying to find its way out of the labyrinth, crying "I'm right, I'm right" all the while. He didn't yet realize that everyone thinks they are all right in their own minds. But even the wisest minds are still terribly limited.

She began to understand that some people were fallen angels who hadn't found their wings while some had. He was just becoming aware that he was an angel. She turned out the light on his side of the bed and wondered when it would be turned on again.

Months later, she would discover an ancient text called *The Perfumed Garden*. In it, she found:

. . . .

RULE #64 Men are warned not to jump out of bed after coming but to hold a woman in their arms and make sure that she has had her pleasure.

. . . .

Too bad Zafeer hadn't read it. Things might have turned out a bit differently.

CHAPTER 43

THE MARQUIS DE SOCKS

After Orlando was late for their date, and she posted the pic of herself with two handsome strangers on Facebook, the black-haired one 'friend requested' her. When she began to examine his profile, she was impressed. Cello, guitar, piano, voice, camera, both director and photographer. A true renaissance man.

Tonight they were finally going to hang out. She couldn't wait. Weeks of studying his pictures had kindled quite an appetite—literally. She headed for a local café and ordered more food than any woman should. When she finished her mountain of bruschetta, fennel salad, meatballs and cappuccino, she told the waiter in Italian that she wanted to have *qualcuno*—some*one* for dessert—instead of *qualcosa*, some*thing*. He was highly amused. She giggled at the *faux pas*, more likely a Freudian slip.

Artemisia was almost intimidated by Gustavo. Her early attempts at flirting were too strong, too 'MYLF' (Mother

You'd Like to Fuck) he told her later. The Italians, like the French, are not above insulting a woman, even if they want to fuck her. Maybe especially if they do. But other than making her feel a bit crass, he was complimentary…loved her music, her singing, her beauty, all of it. Even her breasts, which he knew were 'enhanced' even before seeing them unclothed. No one ever knew.

"They are very well done," he said, "but I can always tell."

Perhaps this is why he made her nervous. He saw things. He looked, stared into.

He held her body in front of him and played her like a cello. "There will be photos later," he said.

After playing music they popped down the hill for some Chinese food and a porno shot. They conquered the hill coming back up like world class climbers. They gazed at the fountain and plotted future escapades to be captured on film.

Back at her apartment, he wanted to talk and talk. At that point of a night, Artemisia wanted to get naked, kiss, touch, climax. He didn't want to kiss. He didn't want to fuck. He was bored with fucking and kissing. He wanted to do different things, but, she convinced him. She could be very convincing when she wanted to be.

At times Gustavo looked like a total nerd with glasses and a pudgy midsection. But in bed, with his glasses off and his hair down, he looked like a 19th century poet, reclined on a four-poster in his ladies chamber, yet ready to jump out the window and scamper off on his horse if needed. He kept his sword handy but hidden. He fit in perfectly with her visions for her new life, in a brick-faced apartment with iron rings in the wall for doing dominating deeds. Still, she felt a bit intimidated by his manner, his beauty…he even had a "beautiful" cock (his words)…half of it was dark brown, almost purple, and the other half very pale. In this light it looked like a chocolate and vanilla concoction rising out of a fluffy furry bed. How she loved hair in the right places, not on the back or upper arms, but where it is supposed to be—belly, chest and genitals. Then she looked down.

"Are you wearing socks in bed? White socks?" She laughed and relaxed a little. She never would have thought such an elegant man would be wearing dirty gym socks, certainly not in these circumstances.

He placed her before him, just so, and tasted her in a manner she had rarely been tasted in. She felt like a delicacy to be devoured, an oyster on a half shell. But somewhere in the midst of her semi-intoxicated throes, his hand went in, and in, and up. It pressed against her somewhere strange. She felt as if she needed to pee.

"Relax," he said. "When you feel as if you need to pee, it's not pee. Just let it go."

She tried to relax through the pain. It did hurt less but still hurt. As she got hotter, his hand would go faster and harder.

"Put your hand here," he said.

She put her hands on her belly and could feel his fingertips on the other side of her own skin. It was the most bizarre sensation.

"I love the squirting," he said. "Feel this. This is all you."

The towel she'd placed beneath them was drenched. When she and Bron had made love in her van, the same thing had happened, but there was so much of it, she thought they'd spilled a bottle of water. And there had been no pain that time.

Do I like pain? she asked herself while he was doing it, and several times the next day, once she finally awoke at almost 15:00.

"How was it?" asked Kyra online, for she knew that Artemisia had been anticipating this date for a while.

"I feel as if I've been with the Marquis de Socks and I was head sock puppet," she told her.

Artemisia still wasn't sure how she felt about pain, but she noticed she was very relaxed, very calm. She sauntered down the hill to Trastevere, her scarlet lipstick on such a sunny day saying it all,

"I am a bad girl, *una ragazzaccia*."

· · · · · · · · · · · · · · · · · ·

RULE #65 There is such a thing as female ejaculation, despite what you may have heard, and it is not the same as an orgasm.

· · · · · · · · · · · · · · · · · ·

CHAPTER 44

PERSEPHONE IN TRASTEVERE

She woke up to a message from Zafeer asking her to delete his photo from her profile. This was after several awkwardly polite messages that she didn't pay much attention to. She blocked him. She rarely blocked people but when she did it felt so good she wanted a cigarette afterward. She had no time to waste on manipulators. But she did have,

. . . .

RULE #66 Sometimes when people don't get what they want, they will try manipulation to keep you in their life. Don't allow it.

. . . .

She was not the Statue of Liberty for the dysfunctional: "Bring me your tired, your poor, your befuddled masses, your broke, your depressed, your narcissistic wankers." Still, it made her sad. She felt like wallowing in a big bath of pity, so she walked to the bar and got a cappuccino and cornetto to go. They weren't used to 'to go' so they gave it to her in a plastic cup meant for cold drinks. She felt like she was drinking cancer, although it tasted delicious. She decided to visit her favorite fountain in all Roma, one of her favorite spots. It was too high to be reached easily from the touristy places so it was one of the cleanest fountains in the city. She watched a lone duck enjoying an exquisite bath in the blue water dappled with sunlight and felt the reassuring warmth of the morning sun on her back.

She needed reassurance, for she was sad. She was tired, and she was worried, for she was bleeding again and her money was almost out. She was sad because people acted out of insecurity and selfishness, instead of compassion and confidence. She was sad because some people expected too much of her, while others underestimated her capabilities. And both parties tended to act out this fantasy on her, to lash out. She was sad that despite all these lovers, she had no one to spend her last weekend in Rome with. They were all busy people with lives, some of them had girlfriends, while her girlfriends had husbands or families to spend their free time with. She was alone with her thoughts, even her daughter had no time to talk to her and she missed Elle terribly.

Work done for the day, all she wanted to do was sleep. Instead, she forced herself off the couch and down the hill to Trastevere, the cool heart of Rome. She'd been invited out, but he wanted her to travel across town to meet him. She did not like cars or most modern transportation. Keep her on her feet until she could fly. Anyway, she wanted to stay in this borough, her burrow. Walking alone, she almost slipped into despair, but then grabbed herself deep within and proclaimed her gratitude.

"I have friends, I have talent, I have work *e sono libera*—I am free." And just like that, she was.

She saw Jermaine who offered her delicious fruit and real African coffee. As the sky darkened, she strolled to Piazza Santa Maria and sat on the fountain steps to watch a new fire dancer. One more stroll brought her to Piazza Trilussa, a popular meeting place and hangout. It always resembled an amphitheatre, with a large fountain reigning over a wide set of stairs which were almost always occupied by dozens if not hundreds of weary or horny travelers and locals, looking out onto the Tiber and the constant stream of souls coming off the Ponte Sisto footbridge. Usually there was a strong odor of piss in the air and a carpet of broken glass underneath, breaking any magic spell it might have held over Artemisia's imagination. But tonight it *was* an amphitheatre—and the piazza was transformed into a mythical Greek land where Persephone, Hades, Demeter and Death all danced about on stilts. Flames and fireworks shot out from torches, in time with the dramatic music which enfolded the crowd in its grip. Persephone's lightness, beauty and innocence were irresistible to the dark lord, and because she was a loner, she was easy pickings. Hades abducted her and brought her to his underworld kingdom. Far from hating him for it, Persephone grew to love Hades, to embrace his darkness. For the rest of her life, she spent half the year with him below ground and the other half above, reunited with her loved ones and the sunlight she needed to keep her own light alive. It was a beautiful spectacle.

Artemisia had never felt more like Persephone, except that she was dark and there was no Hades for her. As innocent as she once was, that was now just a memory, just a dream. Too many people tried to put out her light. One can only fight so many battles before innocence is lost. Once it is gone, it is gone forever. She was now Queen of her own underworld. At times it was terribly lonely, but she did not think she could fly any other way. Her black wings would only be clipped and useless. She was free to go down to the dark side and free to come back to the light, whenever she wanted.

Gustavo had said "Trastevere hugs you every time."

Sometimes it did more than hug. It laid you down in its bower, embraced and grabbed you. It kissed and it bit. Never too rough, but never too tender. Too tender would be boring. She returned up the hill with more energy than she came down. This night Trastevere embraced her beautifully.

. . . .

RULE #67 We need both light and shadow.

. . . .

CHAPTER 45

ME TOO/THE MALE BRAIN

She went to Trilussa not realizing she looked like a mess, until she caught her reflection in a window. She felt compelled to buy something, popped into Acid Drop and bought a little black dress. She put it on and went out into the street still adjusting her straps. She turned to see Leonardo staring at her from behind his bar. The doors were wide open, his view was straight to her, a beam of light emanating from his eyes to her figure. She gave him a cursory glance and smiled to herself. She carried on, passing Orlando.

"*Ciao* Orlando," she said, conveying nothing more than what she felt…friendly.

His handsome but not very intelligent face looked a little frightened by her presence at his work place. It was kind of impossible to avoid, being on the edge of Piazza Trilussa. She kept moving. These boys, she did not care what they thought. She walked around happy but hungry and found the one she'd been looking for all week. The handsome waiter that looked like a new and improved Tom Cruise. Daniele fed her delicious salmon crustini and took her number. She floated home on air, feeling stronger than she'd felt in weeks. She showered, got dressed again, cleaned her house, and waited. Once 1AM came around she was convinced he lost her number. She fell asleep waiting for the handsomest man in Rome to take her out on his scooter, missed the doorbell, the phone call and her date. She woke at 5AM to a message sent hours before: "I'm here."

Far from being upset that she fell asleep and missed her date completely, she was just happy she no longer felt like she was going to have a heart attack just because a boy looked at her. Little Rita had come a long way. If a pretty boy looked her way, Rita could only giggle and look down. Some would be cruel about it, others would be kind, but they were always above her. She was a 'less than' girl; someone to be amused by, pitied, even in some cases, reviled. She, in turn, resented boys. Those that got grades lower than her got more praise because they were boys. Her mother told her that her brother would go to college but that she would get married and have babies. That would be her job. She was a child prodigy but that was beyond her mother's comprehension. So in her family it was the boy that got the vote of confidence in his intellectual capabilities. And he went forth with that knowledge. Like many do.

It was not the fault of boys that they were raised this way, it was the responsibility of the parents. She didn't know if this was still going on, but many of the men she met, young men, tried to dominate her. They had a sense of entitlement she could never have.

She was genderless in so many ways and often gender blind. She didn't care about it. We were all spirits clothed in temporary flesh, the spirit is what mattered. There was a woman—Artemisia guessed she was a trans woman—who worked in a pub not far from her. She was very sexy, very attractive, precisely because she didn't know her gender. She had a strong deep voice. She looked all woman but sounded all man. This was intriguing. Artemisia would date this person.

Famous author Steve Silberman had once told her that she was "a gay man trapped in an Aspergirl's body"…he had no idea how right he was. She used to take Rasputin, make love to him, use him and even abuse him a little until he crawled up the stairs exhausted, practically pleading for mercy. He loved that about her. Maybe the men she needed to be with needed to be a little bit gay. Her anima/animus was too well-balanced for macho types to feel comfortable. Instead they felt competitive.

. . . .

RULE #68 People with androgynous sexuality may need partners who are the same.

. . . .

That would explain her compatibility with Bron and also, Rasputin, who despite his outward denial, privately longed for a trans lover and allowed Artemisia to play that role with him.

The next day Daniele wrote again. He wanted to see her. He arrived wearing a ridiculous shirt with beer bottles on it and carrying enough pizza to feed a family of 12. But his film star face, his gentle eyes. He knew who Jeff Buckley was. 'Hallelujah' was his favorite song. Hers too. She took him to her favorite fountain and view—it was his too. He took her to an even higher spot on Gianicolo Hill and they drank prosecco—their favorite—and nibbled *aperitivo* while looking out over Roma and their favorite building, Altare della Patria. They both loved to swim.

"I live by the sea," he said. "Come swimming with me."

She said yes, but of course she knew it would never happen. He was all male. Yet, she laughed at all the *'me toos'* she uttered in her head like some sort of vapid teenager. And at how two so very different people could have the same likes. He was the kind of boy that would have hated her back in Cheektowaga Central. But in return, she would have looked down on him. Women with Aspergers can be very haughty, herself most of all. Or maybe it is that they were too similar. They both had male brains. And that is what macho men sensed and were uncomfortable with, and felt competitive with. So no matter how it looked from the outside and no matter how great the sex was, the men felt almost gay being with her.

She loved Daniele's body. Not tall, not skinny, nice size penis, and a little bit of a furry belly, her favorite. Not for looks, but for feeling.

The Tinman once told her, "Men with a belly make better lovers."

"Why?" she asked him.

"We generate the heat," he said and rubbed his own generous stomach with a wry grin.

It took a while to find their rhythm but once they did, once she let herself go, she came for ages, multiple times. She did that with Zafeer too. These men didn't believe her when she told them, they didn't know what that was like. For her, it was like riding a wave of bliss, a wave that could pull you under and kill you. But she had become an excellent surfer. Daniele left in the morning and she doubted she'd ever see him again. She felt a bit like what she thought a gay man must feel when he got a 'straight man' to sleep with him. Like she scored, like she tricked him a little. It was naughty, but it was fun.

Anyhow, most men don't want what they've already had. And she was beginning to be that way too.

She booked her rooms in Athens for the next phase of her journey and skipped down the hill to Piazza Trilussa. Jermaine was giving Orlando killer looks from across the piazza. Somehow he found out they'd dated. She begged him to see that she needed a big brother. She hoped that she got through. Clearly she needed protection if she was going to live such a life. She bought herself a beer and mooched a smoke. Reckless but still wreckless, she danced up the hill until her breath failed her and she slowed to a steady climb. The heart that was broken too many times was now fearless and strong, yet would always have that one little potentially fatal flaw. She now believed that she would someday die leaving Trastevere, climbing this hill, a smile on her face, little black dress on her body, someone else's ciggie dangling in her hand. But what better way was there to go?

CHAPTER 46

HELMETS

She arrived in Athens exhausted but had to make the rounds to her old haunts around Acropolis. Afterwards, she Ubered back to the squalid little room she'd foolishly booked on Airbnb. She activated her Tinder account before falling asleep, put The Smiths on YouTube and woke, ten songs later, to several messages. It was her choice, really. She chose Helmut, one month out of a relationship but completely over it, or so he said on Tinder. She decided not to do her hair or look too fancy. She had been pointed out and laughed at earlier by a Greek couple and wanted to avoid looking pretentious.

It was a mistake. Helmut looked extremely handsome when she met him in Monastiraki Square—nice shoes, cool dark blue shirt, pressed grey trousers, groomed black hair and soulful dark eyes. He'd made an effort. They went to one of the rooftop bars that had a stunning view of Acropolis and Parthenon. All the women there, too, had made an effort. Artemisia felt scruffy, but he seemed at first, to be riveted only to her, to her face. For a minute, she fell a little bit in love with this fresh young soldier. (She reminded herself of the Marilyn

Monroe character in *Some Like It Hot* when she said, "I fall in love every time.") Good looking men, smart ones, who dress well, are eloquent, bilingual if not multilingual, these things are rare anywhere. But add a nice smile, a great body and, best of all, an open mind, and you have a real prince. In women, these things are much more common.

He touched her enough to prove his confidence, he was charming, the conversation and the feeling flowed like the delicious cappuccinos they started with and the ouzo which followed. But she was hungry, she needed food.

"I think you want this night to continue, but I need to eat something, or I will faint." Artemisia wanted to find out if this man would buy her dinner. So, she asked him. "Will you buy me dinner?"

He balked a little. She did not think that a woman should ever pay on dates. Her mistake, if there was one, was in telling him that.

"The amount of money women have to pay on makeup, hair products, lotions, potions, perfume, waxing, plucking, shaving, clothing, refining themselves to the point where a man notices them above the crowd is staggering."

He didn't agree with her. "They should not live outside their means," he said. "Men can love women who are plain, it is not how beautiful you are."

Theoretically true, but it was still a little hypocritical. They met on a dating site which, of course, like all dating sites, was all about looks, at least initially. She looked around the bar and there were beautiful women as far as the eye could see; most with men, but others with their girlfriends, for the most part hoping to catch someone's attention. And she couldn't help but notice that he had begun to stare at one of them while talking to her, more noticeably once he'd had an ouzo. Once upon a time, she was a cool chick who pretended not to mind, but let's face it. If a man is staring at other women on your first date what would he be like after a month or a year?

She felt a little sad because she fell out of crush with him at that moment. And because the conversation had made him a bit stern and macho. She went back on her self-promise and offered to buy him noodles from *Street Wok*, her favorite cheap eats in town. She still liked him well enough to want to see the smile back on his face. Artemisia would be an amazing boyfriend. They rode his motorcycle through Athens, the edges of her little black dress flapping in the breeze, an occasional squeal escaping helplessly from her mouth as he popped a wheelie. She grabbed him from behind, his thick leather almost reassuring in her hands, while she gripped him tightly with her thighs, not sure if she was doing it right. But the whole time she was conscious of the fact that he saved the helmet for himself. That said it all.

Still, the ride excited her. She wanted him now. He wore the other kind of helmet when they had sex, which was good, lasted a long time, and would have been hot. But just when she was getting into it, he began to call her *bitch*, and *whore* and *putano*. She tried to protest but he didn't stop calling her names the whole time. She was shocked at first, never having experienced this before. It was distracting, almost funny, if it weren't disturbing. She decided to use it in the moment so that she could finish without being frustrated for the rest of the night, but consciously decided in the middle of the act, that she would not subject herself to it again. There were enough men in the world who knew that you could be a very good person and a very sexual girl at the same time. Was there a woman who really enjoyed being called 'whore' while she was fucking a man? Artemisia didn't know, maybe she should ask a few, do a survey. It just made her think he had issues.

RULE #69 If a man is calling you names during sex and you don't like it, tell him to stop. If he doesn't, you stop.

Of course all these rules are based upon the hope that the man isn't a violent lunatic, or that you *can* stop. Artemisia's ass could be on fire and she probably wouldn't stop till she had an orgasm.

She also realized something else.

RULE #70 If you are on a drinks date and you become hungry, end the date. Or buy yourself something to eat where you are. Don't ask him to buy you dinner.

If your date doesn't offer to buy you dinner, he's not worth your time, or he needs more time to think about you.

The next day Helmut messaged her several times, mainly to say that he was bored. Artemisia was never bored. Clever people can always use their own thoughts to entertain them. She did not write back.

RULE #71 If he writes to you and says "I'm bored, I'm depressed, I'm broke, etc." and you're not even in a relationship, run away. You are not a children's entertainer.

THE BIG BANG

This was a bit of a surprise. Another Tinder date. A Greek actor named Socrates, who looked like a cross between Dermot Mulroney and Ross from *Friends*. They met at the square, like everyone always did. Women stood under the Metro sign, staring at their phones, studying the photos of their blind dates. Tinder was sweeping the world. Artemisia realized how stupid they looked so she wandered away from the sign and scanned the area to see if he was doing the same. She saw a few men looking—no, that wasn't him. She looked at his pic on her tablet once more. He was exceptionally handsome and slightly unusual, there would be no mistaking him.

At last. She walked towards him, he gave her a cursory glance, walked right past, and headed for the sign.

He turned back, "Artemisia?"

She felt old. She never felt this way meeting men but she did this time. He was so handsome, so comfortable in his body. She had just bought a new dress minutes before to add to her confidence, but now she was only noticing the freckles on her arms, her imperfect skin.

This will be the shortest date ever.

They went upstairs at the 360, another place with a stellar view of Parthenon. She relaxed. Since there was no sexual tension, she could be her intellectual, goofy self. They immediately tucked into a good conversation. He was an actor, but not like her experience of actors in the past. He was interested in many things, many subjects. He wasn't interested in getting attention for his looks or even his talent. He was interested in things that interested him. She relaxed a bit more. Like her date of the previous night, she noticed him clocking beautiful blondes. What was it about those creatures? To her they looked unfinished. She liked dark. Anyway, they talked. And talked. And then, at some point, he grabbed her hand. She felt like he was playing at something.

The bill came. She expected him to buy her drink. He expected her to buy her own.

"If a man invites me, a man pays."

"So you'd pay if you invited me?"

"Of course," she responded.

"Check your phone," he said.

Fuck. She was the one who invited him. She would have to watch that in the future.

He lived with his parents. Greece had been hard hit, but he said that wasn't why. "I work as an actor a lot. But I don't want to do shallow projects that don't fulfill me."

She wanted to believe him—she believed that he believed himself. He was honest, very intelligent, full of ideas.

"I"m writing a guide to life. An A-Z," he told her.

She told him she already did and it was published. Maybe she shouldn't have. Drinks paid for, they decided to go for a walk around Acropolis.

"My whole family thinks they have Aspergers," he told her.

No way, she thought…at first.

As they walked and the sun set, he grabbed her ass on the dark path between the ancient Agora and Aeropagus Hill. "Not my best feature," she said. "I have writer's butt."

"That's an excuse."

"It's not an excuse but a reason."

"Using that logic you might as well blame everything on the Big Bang as that was the origin of everything."

Her less-than-perfect ass was the result of the Big Bang.

They stopped. Lovers occupied each and every boulder they saw glowing slightly in the moonlight. They found their own rock. He had already been kissing her. A lot. He wanted to fuck her right then and there but she liked talking to him and wanted to lie with him so she invited him to her shitty little hotel room in a bad neighborhood north of the city center.

Another motorbike ride, but this man was more careful, more concerned for her safety. They bought a couple of beers and went up to her room. The intellectual connection they'd established carried over into sex. She couldn't kiss him enough, she couldn't put him inside of her enough, even though his penis was big and perfect. His body was long and lithe, not too muscular or sinewy, but not in the slightest bit fat. He fucked her so hard the bed moved, hell the earth moved. She wanted to cry out so many times but kept shushing him to not slam the bed around. At the same time, she didn't stop him. He brought her into multiple orgasm mode almost immediately. She stayed there for a very long time. They did it long into the night and then did it again. The second time he came on her tongue. Bitter, not what she expected and not something she did, ever.

Her sheets were cheap and scratchy so she cut open a dress that had started to go nappy and spread it out for a sheet but she ended up sleeping on his chest all night, like a kitten or a baby. She slept very well, waking a few times to fix the shawl they were both using as a cover. But each time, she fell blissfully back to sleep. She dreamed that she invited him to a 'full moon party' and awoke unsure if that meant anything.

When he woke, he was happy, full of energy, cheerful and of course horny. She hated morning sex so she happily encouraged him to jerk off. He did, with no self-consciousness whatsoever. She liked this man. A lot. She didn't really want him to leave, unlike her other dates. The only thing she felt after he left, was a little bit in love and a little bit sad because she knew the hammer would drop and the truth would soon be revealed. That there was no way they could have a relationship.

A message from him: "I'm feeling really wonderful about you."

Yes, but he didn't know. When he found out, and it ended, she would blame it on the Big Bang.

She didn't hear from him for many hours, except for one message that said, "Let's talk tonight."

She was triggered, suddenly, without warning. The darkness that she had kept at bay with her new lifestyle sprang out of the shadows like a bogeyman that was waiting for the light to go out and mommy to close the door. She was paralyzed with terror, not breathing properly. Her head spun. The man on the other side of the wall in her shitty hotel hadn't shut up since she'd come home and he was sending her into meltdown territory. She needed to work, to think, to play but all she wanted to do was drink. She didn't get like this anymore. What was wrong with her? She dared to love, she dared to dream, she dared to care just for a moment. When would she learn that was never going to work? Tears which were so rare since she exorcized the demon of a bad romance from her soul, sprang forth, the well of illusion clearly not dried up yet. Maybe it was linked with her sexuality and as long as that was still a flowing river, Illusion would be the fog her boat of Reason sailed through. Men like him were Sirens. Beautiful Sirens, puncturing the fog but hiding something far worse…the rocks of Reality. Who said Sirens were all women?

And the fact that he was Greek made it all the more perfect.

She rented a two-bedroom apartment, with a large balcony. "For us," she told him in a message.

"You made me so happy with that message," he replied. "Us."

"See? You had nothing to worry about," she told herself.

He moved in with her on a Monday night, after a long mysterious weekend with no communication. He arrived dirty and tired after an exam, carrying a scruffy backpack and nothing else, no gift for her. She poured him some wine on the large balcony and began to talk, to tell him some things about herself. He made himself at home on a bench and then almost immediately proceeded to contradict, even insult her. Cryptically, subtly and then not so subtly. At first she thought she was imagining it, but after several minutes, it was clear that it was both real and relentless.

"Why do you keep arguing with me, telling me I'm wrong? I'm telling you about my life, my thoughts. Things that I know to be true because they are my experience."

"I never said the word 'wrong,' it's all in your imagination," he said smugly and sipped her wine looking pleased with himself.

She tried to agree with him, did everything she could to spin things in his favor, still he still found a way to oppose her.

"It's late. Let's go to bed," she suggested.

They fucked, but the magic was gone. As soon as it was over and he uttered some words, they were contrary once more.

"Tell you what. *I'm* going to use the word wrong and say the only thing I was wrong about tonight, was you. You need to leave now. Go home."

He left at 2AM. He'd been there less than five hours. And she was left stranded on the rocks.

RULE #72 Don't move in with someone after one date. Duh.

CHAPTER 48

THE BEGINNING OF THE END

It happened finally. What Gustavo called boredom with sex. She didn't know how it happened exactly, maybe just the sheer stupidity of the last couple of men she was with: the *putano* mutterer, the stay-at-home-Socrates, the ill-equipped American professor, who did not even inspire a chapter.

She was bored. And going back to Rome. Home sweet Rome. She decided it was time to see Leonardo, talk to him. Tell him they were friends. She had so many lovers since him that he dwindled in importance, yet he was still special in a way. He was there, behind his bar, polishing glasses. She asked him how his trip was, with his *ragazza*.

"Really good," he said with that kinky smile and hair to match.

"Really?" she asked rhetorically. "We're going to be neighbors again, so we'd best be friends."

"I'm leaving in ten days for the south, I'm going home to live."

Leonardo was leaving. She felt her heart sink. "What about *la tua ragazza?*" she asked.

"I am bringing her," he said.

She was happy for him of course. But she still felt the heaviness of loss. The heaviness of knowing that there was no one who wanted to live with *her*, to whisk her away to their village. To introduce her to their mama. And she hated change.

She went to see Jermaine.

"One of my toyboys is leaving and I don't like it when people leave."

He was still bothered that she slept with Orlando.

"How did you know?" she asked him repeatedly.

"It's an African thing."

"I like you because we are on the same level spiritually."

He scoffed. "Pffft. You are not on the same level as me."

Artemisia just looked at him with open eyes. *So be it. If he thinks he's above me then there's no reason for me to stay friends with such a man.*

"I just want to have sex with you," he shouted loudly across the Piazza as she walked quickly away. "This is my life!"

She would not speak with Jermaine again. Ever. She went to see Luciano, whom she liked since she first stumbled into Mr. Brown's asking what a porno shot was and he gave her a free one.

"I am in the market for a new toyboy."

She drank her shots slowly and seductively. Luciano swore fealty to the promise of being her next one. She found out when he was free and they made plans to speak. On her way home, she introduced herself to Yuri, the Ukrainian street singer with the voice of an angel. He promised they would meet tomorrow. Admittedly, she was a little frantic. It's not that she would miss Leonardo, she was just sick of meeting men who already loved someone else; from Rasputin on up, every single one of them had been in love, and she had been just a transitional girl, a bit on the side…

She woke refreshed. It was a new day. She showered, got dressed, felt like a new woman. She had a date with Yuri and wanted to look hot. She had new shoes. She put them on, walked round the edge of her bed to smooth the blankets. It was a little studio but she wanted it to look perfect. Her shoe got tangled up in a bit of bedsheet. She fell forward, hit the ground hard and heard a loud 'snap.'

"Oh my god oh my god oh my god!" she shouted, cradling her right elbow.

She stood up, felt it, looked at it. It was not bent in any strange shape, but it was not right. As the moments wore on she realized something was wrong. In more pain than she could ignore, Artemisia went to the hospital, but there were too many people there. It seemed like all of Rome had injured themselves that day.

"Fuck it," she said, went to the *farmacia*, threw a bandage on it, and went home. "As long as I can play guitar, fuck, and type, I'm happy."

Despite the pain in both her elbows (for both were damaged) she and Yuri had a wonderful first date. They played for each other.

"I had no idea you'd be so good," he said.

He stroked her back as she lay sleeping and made her coffee in the morning. He left that very day for a music gig. He'd be gone a week. When he returned, they made a date to watch a film at Piazza San Cosimato. He sent gifs of horny kittens and told her he wanted to see her before the movie because he couldn't wait to make love to her.

She and her bed were made ready. But the time passed and it got later and later. A message: "Sorry, I'm running late. Go to the movies without me and I'll meet you there."

It's not like he had a day job. He'd already been late for their first date and now, after getting her riled up with promises of hot sex, he said "go to the movie alone"? She'd dealt with too many disappointments lately. Too many teases.

"Fuck off," she told him. They would not speak again.

Artemisia became convinced Jermaine worked some African *juju* on her because she would not go out with him. Curses only work if you believe in them, but unfortunately she did. After watching *The Shining* at an outdoor screen alone, surrounded by couples, she walked down the street like a tourist with a beer in her hand and a dazed expression on her face. She headed for the only thing guaranteed to cheer her up: Luciano and porno shots. As if part of some anti-Artemisia conspiracy, he announced what a lovely day he'd had by the sea with his girlfriend and how he recommended it, only days after he'd offered to be her next lover. He must have told his co-worker of her needs, for an unattractive blonde barkeep peered at Artemisia hungrily from behind the taps like a starving orphan. Disgusted, she left.

· · · · · · · · · · · · · · · · ·

RULE #73 Never make a toyboy or lover out of your fave barista, waiter or bartender.

· · · · · · · · · · · · · · · · ·

Very similar to the 'don't shit where you eat' folk wisdom of the US.

She felt adrift, stranded, without berth or harbor. Had Artemisia gone to the edge of civilization, to the edge of the arctic circle of love and nothing was before her but an icy, pitch black wilderness? She didn't know. Maybe this is why couples stayed together. They knew that life without love was a dark hell.

Oh well. Hell she could handle, but boredom, that was another thing entirely.

CHAPTER 49

THE SCOUNDREL

Artemisia was flying from Rome to Athens. She got off in Belgrade to switch planes, when before she knew it, a card was thrust into her hand and a voice said, "Add me, my name is Cesare. I work in film and you have a face for movies."

He was handsome. Charming Roman curls and big blue saucer eyes, beguilingly innocent looking. They chatted very briefly, before he was dragged off to a connecting flight, by an amused woman Artemisia presumed was a work colleague.

Having a similar opinion about herself, Artemisia had no problem believing him. It didn't occur to her until the next day that it was probably just a line. Her constant gullibility never ceased to surprise her. She was left wondering if he was a total player, or just a normal young man, using whatever tool was at his disposal. Or did he actually mean it? The latter was unlikely. She did know that she wanted to see him again.

She was left with a Hobson's Choice: Choosing to believe in something you know to be false in order to get something (or someone) you want, or pointing out that it is and looking like a bitch, or worse, insecure.

She had a look through his profile pics on Facebook, the social media platform of the day. Cesare looked unceasingly handsome in photos that played up his movie job, where he stood alongside the likes of Kevin Spacey and Johnny Depp. While she was trawling his profile for clues to his age and personality, he found and friended her. Her ability to be incognito had passed. He would now know the horrible truth. One trip down Google Road and his illusion would be shattered. He would be faced with the same dilemma as she. He would almost certainly put her in the 'MYLF zone.' Any chance for a peer relationship would be over. Gustavo had already called her his MYLF and Artemisia did not like it one bit. Men were never dylfs.

That was weeks ago. Cesare was finally back from Cyprus and contacted her the day he returned. He seemed unabashedly eager. There was no way he would be late, or not show up at all.

But it started with "Darling…can we make it later?" and then a bit later and then… "There's an emergency. My three-day-old niece is ill and I'm helping my sister."

As she had done before, she sat in the piazza alone watching all the couples and groups sitting in anticipation of the film, drinking wine, chatting. Cesare said he was still going to come. But by 10PM he hadn't even made his way toward her. Messenger showed her where he was—just over the river near the Pantheon. A place loaded with bars and cafés, but no children's hospital that she or her map app could see. And no one lived there; the area had long been taken over by tourism. Her gut, along with Google maps and deduction, told her he was lying. She sighed and blocked his messages. Being stood up made her furious more than any other thing, except being lied to and stood up.

When he found he could not string her along, he publicly begged on Facebook, for all her contacts to see: "Please, unblock me! Let me explain!"

Such a public show of desperation awarded him a second chance, which he spent telling her that she overreacted.

"I'm sorry but I'm tired of getting stood up by men. You're the third in recent history!"

"That," he responded, "was an inelegant thing to say."

Maybe it was. She could be crass at times.

She wished him well and bid him *buona notte*. She could not go on like this. Summer was overrated. Men were overrated. They were so incredibly selfish and loved to turn it around and tell women how selfish *they* were. Nice ones all were taken. In summer Rome resembled the island of misfit toys. In such an atmosphere, Cesare had held promise, more than most. She was disappointed.

That very night, she plunged into the worst depression she'd had in many months. She drank a whole bottle of wine, deleted her Tinder account, and slept many hours. Morning light did not make her feel any better. She could not eat, felt exhausted although she'd slept long, and wasn't sure what was wrong with her or what to do about it. Her love affair with Rome had cooled as the temperature heated up. Almost overnight it devolved from a romance to a pulp novel to even less. It was disappointing on almost every level since she arrived, tripped, and sprained her elbows. There came a point in every tenacious single woman's dating life where she hit rock bottom. Artemisia had finally hit it.

He wrote again the next day, "See me tonight, please."

Desperate to stay out of depression, she decided to give Cesare another chance. But the moment they met on the steps of the MIUR building, her heart sank. There they were, in his eyes, in his almost invisible sneer: arrogance, dishonesty. But yet he was still, admittedly, a little bit sexy. *In for a penny, in for a pound.* She let him drive her across town to some café in a strange neighborhood, which, except for the presence of a tall pyramid, seemed nondescript and an odd choice for a date.

They talked a bit about their work, their lives. She mentioned using Tinder.

"Tinder," he scoffed. "Is only for sex."

"You say that like it's a bad thing," she joked. He didn't smile. "Not in other cities. People use it for relationships too."

"Well not in Rome."

"How do you know? Do you use it?"

"No," he scoffed. They chatted for a while and it quickly became apparent that he was not at all what she had hoped. He had reminded her of Jonathan, but it was merely a physical resemblance, nothing more.

"That pickup line you used, very effective," she said.

"Yea, it works. Most women are gullible and stupid."

Artemisia immediately clocked him as an enemy of all Aspies. "I'm naive."

"No, you get it. Women often tell me 'you're so cheesy,' but they're the stupid ones. The sexy ones get it, that I'm being like that on purpose."

"So the stupid ones call you out, but the smart ones let it slide. Hmmm. Excuse me, I'll be right back."

She went to the bathroom quickly, to look in the mirror and make sure nothing was out of place, including her brain. His assessment of stupid versus smart, sexy women made her teeth curl, but she wasn't sure if she was putting her own moral stamp on something that was actually normal. When she came back moments later, he was on Tinder.

"Instagram," he tried to claim.

She asked him to take her back to Trastevere. They went for *aperitivo*. She could have gone straight home but believed that the cost of his duplicity was at least a glass of wine and a bite to eat. And, on some level, she always tried to make things right. Even things that were horribly wrong.

At Vin Allegro she told him about some of her recent exploits, knowing she had nothing to lose. And she was beginning to enjoy annoying him.

"You shouldn't talk about this stuff," he said, and looked at the girl at the next table for rescue. The girl seemed impressed with neither of them.

The weather was quite hot and the chicken with the aperitivo may have gone bad. Artemisia immediately got a stomach ache and knew the only salvation was a shot of vodka, ASAP: the ancient way of avoiding salmonella.

She got a shot from Bar Calisto. He didn't want anything. They'd only had one wine all evening and she knew it was because he had a second date lined up for later.

We all know that some men can fuck women they dislike, and celebrate themselves as being 'macho.' But it's different for women. It's never talked about. In the movies, the women who fuck men they dislike are portrayed as 'whores'—they have no standards, they don't love themselves. Artemisia took Cesare back to her place and had sex with him. Her disgust for his shitty little personality had not overridden her desire.

When she was a little girl called Rita, her Barbie and Ken dolls had a very special and specific relationship. Barbie dominated Ken, and would often tie him up and spank him. Although she didn't know exactly what sex was, Barbie wanted to have it with Ken, so little Rita obligingly bumped their nonexistent parts together. It was completely natural to the six- and seven-year-old. A therapist might have said she had penis envy but, in her book, quite a few men had vagina envy, so what did she care?

When Artemisia was done with Cesare, he said something both ridiculous and racist. "I can't believe I just slept with a woman who had sex with an Albanian." He was referring to one of the many conquests she had related at dinner.

"I agree with you on one thing—I should definitely raise my standards." He barely registered the insult before she said, "Leave. And don't let the door hit you in the ass on the way out."

She locked the door, put Eddie Izzard on her headphones and went to sleep laughing. She woke up the next morning, still laughing. She never did this anymore but decided to bend the rules just once and sent a message:

"That was quite a clever stunt you pulled last night so you could get to your second date. I laughed myself to sleep and woke up laughing. You are so CHEESY!"

The man with the worst character gave her the most new rules.

. . . .

RULE #74 There are no bad people, just bad behavior, or people that are bad for you. Except once in a while you may meet a real ratbag.

. . . .

. . . .

RULE #75 Some women can use men, just like men are often accused of using women, and not feel bad about it. Whether or not she should is down to her own morality and evolution.

. . . .

. . . .

RULE #76 It is okay to raise one's standards
and keep them raised. As you evolve, your
tastes and awareness will change.

. . . .

. . . .

RULE #77 It's absolutely okay to walk out on a
date that you are not enjoying for *whatever* reason.

. . . .

To quote Monty Python, sometimes you just need to "run
away."

. . . .

RULE #78 If you really want sex, need sex and
there's no one appropriate, have it with yourself.
Keep a dildo at home—and never forget it's there.

. . . .

As a comedian once said, "at least when I masturbate I'm
having sex with someone I love."

CHAPTER 50

BLIND DATE BOOTY CALL

She had a date. A date with someone she thought she might like. She was afraid that she would fall into bed with them too soon. So, Artemisia decided just to get a booty call to get physical cravings out of the way. She had heard much about these things. She had only done it once before; it wasn't very satisfactory but it served a purpose—it was an American professor in Athens she used to get over her disappointment in Socrates. This prof had very little experience with women, despite being handsome and 34. His propensity to call her 'baby" while they were doing it made her want to laugh but she bit her lip out of kindness.

She found Max on Tinder, and saw that he was connected with several men she knew. She friended him on Facebook, had a good look to make sure he was a local and took a screenshot of his name and pic. She let her best friend, a discreet friend, know he was coming.

"Park out front, ring the bell, I'll drop the keys off the balcony. Bring wine."

He showed up in a BMW wearing nice clothes, sporting tattoos and a cool haircut but no wine. She almost wanted to throw him out because of that, it's not like there were a lot of things to remember. But he quickly put her at ease. They chatted a bit. He seemed a smart, gentle kind of soul. She guessed he was one of the many heartbroken masses that roamed the earth searching for succor where they could get it. Like her.

They got down to business. Things were going fine, and then…

"I wanna fuck you all day," he said, in a whiny little voice that reminded her of an orphan being grateful for gruel.

Distracting, if not downright hilarious, she tried to stay on point. But his cologne was also quite strong and repelling. And then she felt hair on a part of a body she could not stand to feel it: upper arms. It was so gorilla-like in her mind. To her, any man that shaved his balls but walked around with a hairy back or upper arms needed to get his priorities straight.

Do NTs have this problem? she wondered as she gave it her best effort and tried to ignore virtually everything about him.

Frankly she was bored already. *Get done and get off me.*

At this very moment she decided never to have another anonymous booty call for any reason. Ever. Maybe there are some women in the world for whom things like smells and words and textures are not important, but she wasn't one of them.

· · · · · · · · · · · · · · · · · · ·

RULE #79 Blind date booty calls are quite risky under the best of circumstances, but when you have sensory issues each trigger is a bullet that could kill your passion and leave you a bit scarred.

· · · · · · · · · · · · · · · · · · ·

CHAPTER 51

THE CONVENIENT ARRANGEMENT

They met at one of her local cafés, *Ombre Rosse*. Ronaldo wore Ray-Bans that made him look a little bit like De Niro in *Taxi Driver*. This worried her. But almost from the first moment, she realized that he was special. He took her to a nice place and ordered a good white wine. He was a professional football player, retired, still in his thirties. A businessman now. Good head on his shoulders. They talked, laughed, stared into each others' eyes. A lot. She was hungry and although he wasn't, he bought a large tray of charcuterie that she proceeded to shamelessly devour. Artemisia always said she ate like a football player, and now she knew it was more than true.

They chatted about many things, quite comfortably. "Frankly, I'm pleased to find such an eloquent athlete. I've always thought football players were not very bright." She refrained from saying "dumb as shit."

"They're pretty stupid, most of them," he said with a smile. He didn't seem put off by Artemisia's bluntness, or find her at all jarring. "I loved what you said to me...do you remember?"

She did—"*Nice bod, how are the brains?*"

"I have a girlfriend," he announced suddenly.

"Ah." She liked this man. His forthright way of speaking. His honesty.

"She lives in Spain and I only see her a few days a month."

"So what are you looking for?"

"Sex, uncomplicated friendship."

That suited Artemisia well. "And what if your girlfriend knew you were here with me?"

"She'd be hurt."

"And if she did the same thing, found a man for sex, would you be understanding of it?"

"She *wouldn't* do it."

Men. It was inconceivable to him that she might be somewhere at that moment, having Tinder drinks and asking for sex without strings. He was probably right, though. When a woman truly loves a man, she doesn't want anyone else.

They kissed, it was electric. He was a good kisser, not like the other Romans she'd met. He walked her home, to her door. She was tired from her booty call with Max that afternoon and anyway, she wanted to see him again and didn't forget the rule about one night stands.

"Does he come with some extra weight?" asked one of her girlfriends later.

"I didn't see much going on down there."

"I mean, does he have kids? Was he wearing a wedding band, or have a tan line there? Maybe this girl is his wife and he doesn't want to admit it."

That didn't occur to Artemisia. She never remembered to look at a man's hand for a ring, but she almost always checked out his crotch. It was automatic, if discreet (she hoped).

With Ronaldo, she saw no evidence of anything and she was worried she'd be disappointed.

The next day she went to the beach; alone, but he promised to pick her up. She had a lovely time wading in the water, exploring the endless length of beach. It was teeming with people, including a small child openly pissing on the sand, which almost put her off her first day in the Mediterranean/Tyrrhenian Sea. Ronaldo picked her up in a Fiat 500, not a Ferrari, but that kind of experience would have been wasted on her. His GPS led them to a dead end.

"Put your phone away and trust me," she told him. It was fun to know Rome better than a Roman.

They ate at a deserted café and drank white wine again, all one could do in such stifling heat. She was nervous, not at ease like the night before. She wanted him. They went to her place and she was not prepared for what happened next. He was an animal. Almost violent, never very hard, but in a way she was relieved, for his penis was larger than she ever would have suspected. He ravaged her for hours. They even had to take a break because she had an online appointment. He waited quietly on the balcony and then ravaged her some more.

"My girlfriend is coming tomorrow. Is this a problem for you?" he told her after.

"Not at all."

"She leaves again Tuesday. Don't use WhatsApp to reach me, use Tinder."

"I won't need to reach you," she smiled.

It was true. She could be quite happy for a few days without him. And she was not in love with him or anyone. How nice that was. She was however, in love with Roma again. In particular, Trastevere and *La Dolce Vita*.

- - - - - - - - - - - - - - - - - -

RULE #80 Not all athletes are dumb. Let's face it. Some intellectual women might have this preconception and it is simply inaccurate.

- - - - - - - - - - - - - - - - - - -

CHAPTER 52

DADDY ISSUES

Hungry after Ronaldo, she popped out to get a beer and some pizza and to quietly return to her balcony to sip her way to oblivion...with a smile on her face and tranquility in her loins. She couldn't help but smirk after she had sex. And men, they saw, it, they sensed a Mona Lisa in their midst. Maurizio followed her out of the pizzeria and trotted down the street after her. He showed her pictures of his yacht and insisted on buying her a drink.

"Okay, *una birra*. Why not?"

This one was Daddy material. She was very happy with Ronaldo but who knew how long they would last? And he was not the right age to 'father' a girl, meaning take her to the opera, or help with her significant expenses. Maybe this would be the missing piece of the Artemisian puzzle that was her new life. Three men to care for her needs. Some unknown young one for kindness, gentleness, and long slow sessions of sexual pleasure. Ronaldo for animal sex, strange sessions of violence and abomination, aberration and descension into dark places. With him she is chained to a gladiator's cell wall, where with others, like Rasputin, she was the chainer. Maurizio could be the father, and could provide for her materially in a way that she could not provide for herself. He texted her twice that night and again the next morning:

"Have breakfast with me."

Artemisia wanted to make him wait and have lunch instead, so there would be wine and lowered defenses. That way she could get to know his true intentions.

They met at Piazza Farnese where he was waiting in the shadows. His attire was youthful but his glasses and mannerisms were old mannish. They strolled through Campo dei Fiori, what Artemisia liked to call The French Quarter because of the Embassie it housed. They popped into one of the many small but world class galleries there. Maurizio tried to impress her with his knowledge of modern art and his pronouncement of a small collection of *Poliakoffs*. But he took too long in the gallery.

As he spoke with the attendant, Artemisia artfully wiped a smear of her red lipstick off his cheek and said, "It's better to discuss art on a full stomach."

They went into a nearby café. He was severe, his crossed arms and slight insults revealing his insecurity. He was newly divorced and lonely. Looking for a new wifey. Just add woman and stir.

Artemisia told him point blank what she was looking for: "Someone to take me shopping, to the opera, on vacation now and then."

"You are dangerous," he said. "You are the kind of woman I could fall in love with."

"Oh no, not me. I don't want that." Did he not hear her?

They held hands as they walked but it was time to part. She gave him a mild kiss goodbye. "Think about what I said."

Apparently he didn't, judging by the text message he sent soon after which consisted of his address and the words "Please come."

She ignored it. Men don't hear what you say, they hear what they want. Perhaps we all did this, she mused.

She passed him again in the street later, or rather he passed her as she sat at an outdoor café. He was eating bread and shopping for an iron. She was flirting with another handsome sexy bad boy. Poor Maurizio. She didn't think he had what she needed, even if he did want to run for Parliament.

Artemisia used to love the film *Under the Tuscan Sun*. In it a divorced woman travels to Italy and learns how to live, but in the end it is the 'one man for one woman scenario' which prevails and presumably saves her. An English woman she meets there is a typical cougar, beautiful, older, adventurous, but in the end her young lover leaves her and she goes a bit mad, bathing in the fountain, a tragic caricature of Anita Ekberg in *La Dolce Vita*. There were no alternatives in mainstream mythology. Have sex with one man or you will end up alone, crazy, splashing about in a fountain, the laughing stock of the village, however kind the villagers were. Artemisia begged to differ.

· · · · · · · · · · · · · · · · · · ·

RULE #81 She chose to be free, to see whomever she wanted. She chose life on her terms and if someone did not understand it, he did not have to be part of it.

· · · · · · · · · · · · · · · · · · ·

Let him find someone else, someone more right for him.

SEX AND THE SINGLE ASPIE

....

RULE #82 Instead of being the water flowing around the rock, try being the rock. Let others take you as you are.

....

Do not shape yourself to them, nor expect them to shape themselves to you...except maybe in bed. Women have been told, since the dawn of time, what it means to be 'a lady.' Rules created by men's laws: religious laws, political laws, perpetuated by everyone. Perhaps it was necessary once, but,

....

RULE #83 The time has come for women to decide what it means to be a woman.

....

Again and again, Maurizio ignored her words and invited her to his flat or for a beer.

She reminded him of her initial offering: "I'm looking for someone who can show me some of the finer things in life, things I cannot or would not do for myself."

His response: "You want the finer things in life? I wish you the best."

Fine. She felt free. No, she was free. She was fine alone. Someone would have to offer something she didn't have on her own. And it would have to be something pretty special.

CHAPTER 53

INNOCENCE BETRAYED, THEN LOST

She went to a movie alone, and managed to enjoy it. Practically stayed through the whole thing, which was pretty amazing considering she sat on concrete drinking beer the whole time. The film was *Blue Velvet* and so was the sky. The temperature, so stifling inside, especially during the day, couched her calmly and comfortably like angel's wings and she understood where the Italian Renaissance painters got their images from; she felt very close to their image of heaven, if not their idea of god.

A dog slid under a lady's chair and silently, gleefully, licked the open top of her beer bottle. When she picked it up moment's later, Artemisia watched to see if she would know something was amiss, but the woman simply smiled, drank and put the bottle down again. Artemisia decided now was not the time for Aspie honesty and instead surveyed the crowd of kissing couples, good grandsons accompanying their grannies, girls having girl's night, boys standing on the periphery checking their phones for social salvation.

A neurotypical hair-flicker sat too close and proceeded to flick her long brown curls within inches of Artemisia's nose every two minutes, a move that used to send her into meltdown mode. She simply pressed her toes gently into the woman's back the next time she did it and it seemed to send the message: *Stop it.*

She thought about every man that had ever made her sad and not one of them was worth the salt in her tears, in the end. Some had flown across oceans to meet her. Whatever it was they were looking for, she didn't have it.

Artemisia was rethinking her strategy. What had she gained from all this man-izing? Other than some healthy exercise and a few free meals, not much, except perhaps a reputation. She didn't care about that. It was a world of hypocrisy and double standards. It was fine for Cesare to be on Tinder during their date, but not for her to use it at any time. It was fine for all of them to cheat on their girlfriends, but not for her to be the one they cheated with.

She walked down the street in a plain red frock and a passing young nun looked at her in horror as if she had an upside down cross tattooed on her forehead. Artemisia grinned back at her, thinking, *I am not an innocent but nor am I a hypocrite. I am what I am and proud of it.*

The Tree of Knowledge was something you were told to aspire to, in every place but the bedroom and religion. She was a seeker of knowledge and she was always receiving Judgment, even when she was the embodiment of innocence. When she was just eight years old, her sister walked out of the house in a mini-skirt and stuck her thumb up to hitch a ride. Her martyred mom looked out the window and started crying.

"Don't cry, Mommy," Artemisia said. "Everything will be alright."

"You're going to turn out as bad as the rest of them," said her mother.

Artemisia felt like she'd been kicked in the stomach. All she ever wanted was to be a good girl. If she saw someone saying that to any child now, she'd set them straight. And they wonder why some kids go mad, become violent. Children hate unfairness, hypocrisy and bullying. Aspie children particularly.

As she looked back over her life, that seemed to be the moment innocence was betrayed. The rest of her life seemed to be spent trying to hang onto it. She finally gave up and realized it was lost…but that was okay. It was time.

. . . .

RULE #84 To be a woman alone, especially a woman on the spectrum, means you have to be stronger than you ever thought possible and believe in yourself…more than any ideology.

. . . .

CHAPTER 54

DROWNING, OR INTIMACY

Artemisia went to the beach again. Almost immediately she was pummeled and dragged by waves, getting a scraped bottom, lungs full of salt water and a battered image…the lifeguard could barely be bothered rescuing her from the constant barrage of waves that were dragging her like a doll along the sand.

She felt too thin, insignificant. She'd gained 12 kilos after leaving Paris but maybe it still wasn't enough. Maybe it was a warning from the universe. She kept getting hurt, or sick, several times, except when she was with Rasputin.

A palmist had looked at her hand years ago. Her head snapped up quickly, her witchy blue eyes frightened by what they saw. "You're not supposed to be here."

"What do you mean?"

"Did you almost die when you were little?"

"Yes."

"You were supposed to go. But something wants you here."

Yes, but angel or devil, for good or for evil…who knew? She fell down two flights of stairs at 18 months. Choked at age two. Her appendix ruptured when she was three. She was hit by a van at age five and almost drowned at age six. And so on and so on…

Recently there had been several incidents. Doctors wanted to take out most of her organs—ovaries, uterus, part of her intestines. But she walked out of the hospital, crawled actually, and healed herself, enough to be considered away from the crisis zone. She wasn't going to walk around an empty shell. No one lived forever. Not even her.

On the way to the beach, a couple got on the train. The man sat next to Artemisia and beckoned repeatedly for the girl to come and sit on his lap. The train was hot and crowded so Artemisia really hoped the girlfriend would stay put. But she succumbed to her boyfriend's call and sat on his lap. He began to kiss her shoulders, neck and back with big, loud, smacky kisses. Artemisia did not normally mind such things, but the kisses were rather graphic, and the man's lips were just inches from her ears and it just went on and on and on. After several minutes of spit-soaked smacks, she finally could stand it no more.

"Would you like me to move so you can have some privacy?"

She didn't yell hysterically like she might have as a young Aspie, but she made her point. They stopped. The other passengers seemed secretly grateful, or so she hoped. Maybe she was just becoming one of those women. The bitter, lonely kind.

And then, she heard from Ronaldo. "What are you doing tonight? Would you like to drink something with me?"

She hadn't heard from him in days and here he was asking for a last minute date.

I'm busy, she thought, but didn't type it.

"It would be nice to do something besides drink," she wrote. He'd never been cheap before.

"What do you mean?"

Poor man, he thinks I want to be his girlfriend. "You know, like a walk, a show, a museum, a sporting event, a concert. Use your imagination."

Despite her fear of becoming a grouchy lonely old lady, she was tired of the same old same old and was about to give up.

But Ronaldo would not give up. He kept messaging.

She thought for a long while after he left and something had been bothering her. She took a deep breath and typed: "You spat on me."

"What? When?"

"When we had sex."

It was true. He had spat on her vagina while they were having sex. A lot, even after she asked him to stop. The thought of it afterward made her sick. Life was not a porn film. Too many men were getting their idea of good sex from porn.

"I am *so* sorry!"

He seemed truly unaware. Since he was in every other way a gentleman, albeit a savage one, she decided to give him one more shot. They met, he was charming, as usual. They had a lovely time, even if it was just another *aperitivo* date. She was beginning to realize that *aperitivos* were for dates that either didn't care enough to buy you dinner or couldn't afford to. They walked a lot, talked a lot, and then sat by the Pantheon and kissed a lot. Her body liked him more than her mind.

She took him back to hers. He began acting like a dog, kissing like one. He wanted her on her knees so he could take her from behind.

"I don't want that," she objected. "What's wrong with you today?"

"It's the heat, I'm uncomfortable." He certainly looked it. "Can we do it on the table?"

She sat on it for two seconds and said, "I'm sorry this is not working for me."

She'd done it on a table before but it was spontaneous and hot; this felt like a last resort and the ending of a bad movie.

"I don't have to be in love with a man to be intimate."

"It's not intentional, it's my body. It feels like it's cheating."

"You are cheating even if you aren't affectionate," she told him.

His girlfriend lived out of the country. She knew this and she understood his need for someone here. But, when Artemisia had sex, she also had intimacy. There was no point otherwise. She wanted to hug, kiss, see the person's eyes, see their soul a little bit. Maybe that's why some didn't come back. They either thought she was in love, or it just scared them, made them feel exposed. She hadn't fallen in love with any of them, only moments of big crush, like with Leonardo. But they always turned out to be obviously not right for her. Letting go was not an issue. Not with any of them.

Some of these men were good men, but they detached emotionally, completely. That was the thing she kind of knew but now she *knew*. She didn't miss being in love, but she did miss intimacy. She would miss Ronaldo, but he could not give her what she needed.

"Take care of yourself. I hope you find a way to be with your girlfriend all the time."

"I wish you the best in your life, too."

He left. She was fine. It was the best ending of any affair, long or short, she'd ever had. Evolution.

In the morning she thought about Rasputin and why women all fell in love with him. Because, not only did he lie convincingly about being in love, but he threw himself into sex, fully and with intimacy.

. . . .

RULE #85 A true narcissist only cares about his own experience. The aftermath is not his problem.

. . . .

Perhaps this is why most sane men do not feel intimacy, or show it, lightly. Otherwise they would leave a trail of broken hearts.

. . . .

RULE #86 No more cheap dates after the first 'getting to know you' coffee date. At some point, they have to show you that they value you.

. . . .

She had always been so tolerant, so understanding, so patient. But even men she grew serious with always seemed to be broke until it was time to buy themselves a Porsche or something they wanted. Sure, some people don't have a lot of money, but they can still be romantic, make an effort.

CHAPTER 55

TOWERS

She rose early, lonely and fed up with bad boys and bad sex. She went for a walk, drank water by hand out of her favorite drinking fountain, like some sort of sacrament, then climbed the hill to Fontana dell'Acqua Paola. In the early light, she noticed the features of the sculptures much more clearly than usual. Dragons, gryphons, eagles, and an angel that had the exact face of Rasputin, only as she had once imagined him to be, kind and wise instead of drunk, coked up and cruel. For a moment the statue seemed to move. At that moment she realized that this entire sexual adventure had been to prove a point: that she was beautiful and desirable and didn't need him.

Her point was proved. Now what?

Artemisia was having an existential crisis. How could an attractive woman be so lonely...in *Rome*? All her friends were away—no one had told her that Europeans completely disappear in August—for the entire month. Her coffers were emptied from maintaining a house in the US and a life on the road, and she was forced to dine in most of the time now on pasta and not much else. And the other night her Aspergers reared its head in an ugly way when she met Gustavo's friends, but at least she'd had a massive revelation afterwards: she did not like to socialize with both sexes at the same time. All women or all men, she was fine. But put them together and it was like having tea with the Mad Hatter only less comprehensible…she simply didn't know what to say or when to say it.

Artemisia was still ill, sleeping much of the time. She hoped her swollen tummy was just the result of too much pasta; for, as charming as it would be to have a medical miracle, it would not be wise. She was dizzy, her vision was blurry. Objects were taking on that strange, movable, Van Gogh quality. She was having nightmares again; the black Tower from the tarot deck kept appearing in her dreams. This summer she twisted her ankle, sprained both her elbows, and nearly drowned in shallow waters. She half-wondered if the universe was simply telling her to leave Rome. But one had to pick a ground to plant in and although she missed Elle, she didn't miss America enough to live there full time.

Ultimately, it was her own naivete that was killing her, not a particular place, or a person. When someone said "let's do something" she immediately, and always, believed that they meant it. Someone in Siberia could say, "if you come we'll do this project together" and she would go. Once she arrived, they probably wouldn't even remember saying it, instead they would wonder why the hell she was wandering around their village alone, trying to look like she belonged but feeling like a ghost. And when a soul is displaced, well, it *is* just a ghost, isn't it? A zombie.

Believing people meant what they said and said what they meant, this was the root cause of all her problems.

"I love you, I need you, save me."

"I will stay with you forever."

"I'll put you on television. I'll put you in movies. You're going to be a big star."

"You're going to be the first lady of France."

My god, a lifetime of horseshit. When would she stop believing? And who would she be without her naivete? She almost couldn't imagine. For cynics were the ones who slammed doors, they didn't open them. She loved to open doors.

One thing was for certain. Mean men had become repugnant to her. And she was getting better able to see through the thin veneer of charm. To see the ego which sits on the brow, in the curl of a lip, the shadow in an eye; the cutting word designed to make you feel insecure.

She had also dated some very beautiful but shallow creatures. The kind that were in films, on stages, in magazines. The ones who never connected very deeply, when you looked into their eyes, they were only seeing themselves in a reflection. Some were dissatisfied with their lives, their jobs, their beauty, while not realizing it was the having of those things that afforded them the luxury of complaint. They were so used to receiving, often they really did not know how to give.

Why then, was beauty important to her? Well, when you grew up in an ugly home, with ugly furniture, ugly architecture, ugly clothes, ugly manners, ugly conversations and ugly emotions, beauty became paramount. When she was very little, she gazed for hours at photos of outer space, particularly the Horsehead Nebula, and at photos of famous paintings. Medieval art was her favorite, with its skewed perspective, perhaps because it proved beyond a doubt that entire civilizations could have skewed perspectives and not know it.

She too, was guilty of having an inflated ego and skewed perspective. She could be flippant, shallow, and she'd allowed a tiny bit of fame, looks and a once growing bank account to let her think she was on a higher plane than others, that she had finally arrived in that ivory tower after a life that was more like a Thomas Hardy novel than anything else.

She now felt like she had only two real choices: *Be celibate, or have a few lovers so that the weight of her did not fall too heavily on one set of shoulders.* And love no one. For she was too much for any one man, and they would never be enough for her. She was not, as Rasputin had said, a bird: she was a dragon. The winged heart tattooed on her teenage chest was as prophetic as she had foolishly hoped it would be.

. . . .

RULE #87 People, especially NTs, do not always say what they mean and mean what they say. What seems like a promise to you, may be less than a plan to someone else.

. . . .

Especially in social situations, where people are not getting paid for their time, when they cannot be fired for not showing up, you cannot rely on even those you've known a long time, much less someone you've just met.

CHAPTER 56

"GRAB 'EM BY THE PENIS"

They met online. He was a doctor, or so he claimed, from Bombay who lived and worked in Abu Dhabi, and was traveling through Europe. They flirted, they shared sexy but not crass photos. He was stunning, with a body like a Dothraki warrior and a face like an Indian Prince. She made it clear she was a sinner with a brain and he would have to show a little more than the usual clichés or he would not hold her interest or her body. After a day of this, she woke to a message:

"I need naughty women like you to make me go wild."

Oh brother. There were so many things wrong with that statement he might as well have shot himself in the mouth with a poo gun. A woman who was comfortable with sex was 'naughty' like a child. 'Women like you' meant that she was common. He mentioned his own needs, but there was no mention of hers. Such entitlement! If a doctor, a traveled and educated man had these thoughts, what chance did a plumber have, or a delivery man, or a waiter, or anyone? And what chance did the women of the world have in finding respect or an intelligent equal footing? This mentality said,

"Be an ornament and like it. You are here to please ME."

Recently in America there had been an election. The male candidate was caught on film saying "I grab 'em [women] by the pussy, you can do that when you are famous." If the female candidate had said "I grab men by the penis, you can do that when you're famous," there would have been such a furor, not seen since the last red-haired oddity was burned at the stake for allegedly sparking a village-wide case of influenza.

Artemisia had watched a lot of pornography. It had served its purpose but only to a point. Then, it very quickly became clear—it was almost always a kind of rape. It was—even if the women were of age and consenting—always about objectifying the woman. This in itself would not be bad if, in equal measure, women used and objectified men. But you almost never saw this. She had searched. So what happened to the viewers? Both men and women have orgasms, fantasies, that have twisted thoughts clinging to their underbelly, like mussels clinging to the hull of a ship, heading into a fresh lake they will poison.

When she was younger she did find some women-made, women-oriented options. But instead of this growing in popularity, the plethora of hip-hop imagery that was all about tits and ass had only reinforced tradition. This was not a knock of women artists who flaunted their beautiful bodies and sexuality, but the ornaments, to use that word again, that made men feel comfortable in where they were without having to grow forward and upward. Along came a new president, who did precisely the same thing. He said to men: "Be an asshole like me and you can rule the world." And to women, he said, "If you don't like it, it is because you are frigid and ugly," etc. Artemisia was neither frigid nor ugly. But she was bored with stupidity and frightened by barbarity.

She wished she found women attractive, since they were so much easier for her to communicate with on any sort of deep level. She was bisexual for a while, a few different times in her life. She and the one she loved most used to have ménage à trois frequently with women they met online, or in clubs. She was, for a time, very enthusiastic about sex with women, although she rarely did it without a man present. She liked it very much, sometimes she liked it more than being with a man. The softness, the gentleness. But women, like men, are made of tastes and textures and smells and moods and attitudes and it was more complicated to find a woman she fancied than it was a man. She personally had never been in love or obsessed with a woman. And, one day, the attraction stopped. She simply could no longer think of women in this light. She tried once, for Rasputin, but it was not satisfying to her, even though it was a friend she loved and thought was beautiful.

. . . .

RULE #88 We simply cannot force ourselves to be either gay or straight or anything but what we are. We can only push boundaries, experiment and expand.

. . . .

CHAPTER 57

THE SEXUAL SAVANT

She traded in one dark prince for another. She decided to give Tinder one more go, have one more stroll through the gallery of lonely/horny man photos. Arash had lips that Batman would kill for. The kind that a cowgirl could ride like a bucking bronco. He had long curly hair and black eyes that had a light deep within that invited exploration. He was only 30, but his latest pic showed he might be on the threshold of that thing called middle age.

She sensed the moment they began messaging each other that he was a creature like her, an Aspie. They met. She asked him to please not be late. After some of the others, she was a bit touchy on that. He promised to be on time and he was. After a short stroll in which he seemed passive and happy to let her take the reins, they settled in at what was once Leonardo's café, safe to visit now that he was living a seaside life with his girlfriend.

Quickly Arash made it clear that he had some insight into Woman—with a capital W—collectively, as a species. He had made them his special course of study, by studying individuals in depth. He counted his lovers like another Aspie might count the number of train cars that passed by.

"Two hundred fifty-six," he said, without a hint of bragging or deceit.

That was a lot of experience. She sensed she might be in the presence of a *sexual savant*. She had suggested a walk to her favorite spots ending at Gianicolo lookout point, but once they sat down at the fountain a little breathless from the climb, he began holding her hand, touching her red painted toes, all the while telling her casual stories. She reached out, took his hair down and his soft black curls fell onto lean strong shoulders. At that point all she wanted was to be alone with him in her apartment as quickly as possible.

She tried to postpone the inevitable and prolong the anticipation, but sitting on her balcony with him and drinking a glass of wine was now almost pointless.

"We have to go inside or my neighbors will see something they did not expect."

Once inside, she was stunned by so many things about him. She was amazed at his kisses. She'd experienced this with Zafeer, who did this pulsating, sucking thing on her, memorably on her thigh, which drove her wild. Arash did it everywhere, even her eyes, and of course, her mouth.

"Some women need to be kissed here, or here," Arash said, touching her shoulder blade and then her middle back, "but most just need the breasts and the usual places."

"What about men?"

"We're more simple," he said, and touched behind his ear, then his balls.

"What about asses?"

"Most men are afraid."

Arash was right about that. Most pushed her hand away. Part of the reason she'd loved Rasputin was that he threw himself completely into sex, no half measures. He even let her dominate and take him with a dildo. Apart from rare physiological reasons, she was sure that people who didn't enjoy sex just didn't know how to let go. They thought too much. She'd read that about 75 percent of all women never reach orgasm from intercourse alone, without the extra help of sex toys, hands or tongue. And 10 to 15 percent never climaxed under any circumstances. She was glad she was not one of those. Sex, making love, was not a question of technique as much as it was intuitiveness, letting yourself be free.

The size of Arash's penis was unbelievable, especially relative to the thinness of his body. It was perfect, and hard as rock. He was gentle, he was kind and he was skilled. To be with a sexual savant, to be free to receive pleasure without feeling like a victim of violence was such a relief after all the players she'd met this year. Only Bron had been this good. But Artemisia did not feel anything like love for this man. He just didn't invite it, despite telling her that other women had asked him to marry them. She couldn't imagine having anything like a romance with him, but she could imagine sex. Lots and lots of it, with good talks before, after and possibly during.

It was like having her own personal Johnny Depp in *Don Juan de Marco*, except he was Don Juan de Persia. And she was left purring like a happy cat.

"Can I stay the night?"

She thought about it for a bit and smiled, "No, I want to wake up alone."

He didn't mind in the least and left cheerfully.

What a nice freaking change, she thought, and snuggled into her sheets.

. . . .

RULE #89 A man does not have to be violent
or aggressive to be 'manly' in bed. He can be
assertive and gentle at the same time.

. . . .

For perhaps the first time, she experienced total kindness in
bed that was also completely sexually satisfying.

CHAPTER 58

FALLING APART

Arash wanted to see her the next day but she was afraid. Afraid that she would become dependent on him and that he would become bored, or vice versa. She was also tired, not having slept very well. Money problems were robbing her of her rest.

She waited a day and then went to meet him with an unspecified feeling of dread. She liked him, everything seemed good. But she knew on some level, or at least she feared, that she would be disappointed yet again. She chose an all black outfit, believing that he preferred a woman dressed in black. When she saw him, she was pleased to see that they matched, for he too was all in black. They talked about something to do. A movie, some jazz. He liked jazz. How nice it would be to go to Ego Café with a date.

But on the way there, Arash stopped her and said, "Don't waste time, use every moment. Your feelings might change and you might not want to be with me again."

She wasn't sure why he was saying this. "When are you leaving for Iran?"

"August ninth."

"That's in two weeks. That gives us some time."

"But," he hesitated for a moment and said, "I have a woman coming to stay with me August first until I leave. I won't be able to see you."

"Your girlfriend?"

"No, she was but I don't want her. I want you. She just wants to see me one last time."

Screech. Slam. The door was closed. The end of the road was visible and it was only a week away. And the guard blocking it was not a six foot soldier, it was a nubile 22-year-old who was in love with him.

"I want to go home."

"Let me come with you," he pleaded.

They stopped at a mini-mart to buy some wine and bread. And then something strange happened. She began to shake, to cry. She fell apart, right in the Roman mini-mart on the edge of Trastevere, in front of her usual grocer. She tried to stop but couldn't.

They went to her apartment. Arash did his best to reason with her, to use logic, to tell her that it wasn't important. That she was lucky. But she did not feel lucky. This was just more of the same. This was just another disappointment in a long line of disappointments.

If she had sex with him, walked with him, talked, cooked, ate, slept with him every day until the woman came, the ending would be abrupt, violent. For it to end because he had to go and see his family was one thing, but this was quite another. Artemisia pictured long nights alone in bed, missing him while he was fucking someone else five miles away. She just couldn't do it.

She spent the next hour trying to tell him all the sad stories of her life.

He was smoking a cigarette on her balcony, staring at her with those black eyes. Suddenly he smiled a wry grin and said, "Shut up."

Artemisia was stunned. "Did you just tell me to shut up?"

"Yes."

So she did. He left.

Artemisia now believed that the main reason she was chronically single was that she could see the double standard *everywhere*. Men lied about their personalities, jobs, motives. They had girlfriends they cheated on, said they were free when they weren't. They messaged other women on Tinder when she went to the bathroom. They criticized her comfortableness with her own sexuality while they themselves were rampant. They made dates she got ready for and then were hours late. When they were caught out, they said things like "I knew you were smart enough to see through it/strong enough to handle it/cool enough to accept it" etc. They used flattery to keep her compliant. If a woman did a fraction of these things she'd be a Queen Bitch. If Artemisia did a fraction of these things she'd be a Queen Bitch.

Some women said they never slept with a man too soon. Others slept with men on the first or second date and had perfectly good results. Artemisia didn't think that was her issue. She had said, and those who knew her most agreed, people seemed to hold her to a higher standard, and to be quicker to tear her down at the slightest opportunity. For the moment, she decided, she was through with love. All she had learned was that the only women in the world who keep men are either smart women who constantly battle for respect with even the men that supposedly love them, or they have asses you can set a glass on. And she wasn't willing to stick out her nose or her ass on a daily basis for anyone.

RULE #90 The days of second chances were over.

RULE #91 The difference between being hanged and changed is the ability to 'C.' She was forever changed.

CHAPTER 59

E FOR ELUSION

Ediz was a date to get over Arash. She didn't have much hope for the yellow T-shirted man who confessed he'd already gotten himself dinner and a liter of wine. But soon they were chatting away comfortably. She wanted *aperitivo* despite her intentions not to be a cheap date. He couldn't very well take her to Antica Pesa in a T-shirt anyway.

During the meal Artemisia went inside to the bathroom. A man was waiting outside the door for her.

"I don't mean to alarm you but I saw your date do something weird." He described how Ediz opened a packet and appeared to put the contents of a capsule on Artemisia's fork.

She thanked the man and looked in the mirror, thoughtfully washing her hands. It was a serious accusation, but you couldn't be too quick to believe Americans. They were the police of the world, well-intentioned, but fearful thanks to the brainwashing they were all constantly subjected to, on what had become an Orwellian diet of 24-hour news, sensationalized and scored with dramatic, terror-inducing music.

She took a deep breath, went upstairs and said to Ediz: "I am a witch. I see things. I saw you put something on my fork."

"No, I just opened this packet of paracetamol. I have a little headache from the wine." He showed her the packet with the plastic seal and reenacted his supposed crime.

She sniffed and licked her fork. It was clean. "Okay, I believe you."

He seemed genuinely relieved, and nonplussed at her announcement of having preternatural vision. She took him to get porno shots, like she did with all of her dates. Nothing like yummy chocolate to break the ice.

After a bit of walking and holding hands, they kissed. He was only in town for two days, there was no chance of a meaningful relationship. She wanted sex. They went to her place and had it. He was good at oral sex. They copulated but he couldn't cum. He said it was from alcohol and drugs.

"You do have drugs? What drugs?" she asked.

"Ecstasy."

"Did you put some on my fork?"

"No! Of course not."

"I want some."

"Really?" He was surprised.

She asked if it was the same stuff he'd already taken so that she wouldn't be getting something untested.

"Yes, and it's not very strong."

Still, she only took half. They went back to bar San Calisto where they'd met and soon it began to kick in. His Turkish accent became more and more Irish as his jaw got wired from the drugs. It made her laugh. They walked along the river, holding hands, kissing, taking photos. The conversation flowed. He bought a pair of earrings, only needed one so he gave her the other. She quickly re-pierced her right ear, the secondary hole which hadn't been used for years. The "E" was in full force now.

"We need to go dancing," announced Ediz.

They went back to her place where she changed into a little red dress. They took three taxis in search of music and a dance floor, only to find two closed clubs and a really tacky tourist bar filled with teens acting silly. They fled immediately and went back to Trastevere, which was always reassuringly cool despite the absence of actual clubs. Now seriously high, they walked down the crowded *Vicolo del Cinque*.

"That man just raped you with his eyes," he said, glaring at some passerby.

"Are you jealous?"

"Yes." His Turkish accent was now a full-blown Irish brogue.

She was glad, no man had ever been so demonstrably jealous over her before. "You're not Turkish, you're IRA," she joked.

Very late in the night, they climbed Gianicolo Hill, to the fountain. They were almost hallucinating now, the cobblestones seemed to rise to meet their feet. As they sat on a bench, the formidable, silent giant almost took their breath away as it rose before them. Its geysers were stilled, its normally pale blue pool the color of Grecian night. Ediz almost panicked from it all and was grinding his jaw into oblivion.

"Here, let me do something." She put her hands on his head, performed some *reiki* and he soon melted under her touch.

"Maybe it's placebo effect, but it totally worked. You are a witch."

"Told you." And then she told him the truth about what really happened earlier at the restaurant. "That man sitting next to us said you might have drugged me. I didn't want to jump to conclusions."

"Wow," he said, "You were so nice about it. You handled that so...kindly."

Ediz took a picture of a couple that had been struggling to get a selfie. Artemisia marveled that he could hold it in his hands, much less focus. She was deliciously high now. But it was time to go home. She laughed as their feet danced back down Gianicolo Hill while their hands fluttered out to the stars, hip hop pumping from a rooftop bar. Ediz got his music in the end. They had not a care in the world, save for the passing of time saying, *Quick, separate worlds await you.*

They went to bed finally. She told him her age.

"But, you're 32." His face and eyes made it clear he hadn't processed it.

She felt bad for him. The Italians, the French, the Iranian, the Kurd, most had not minded. But this one, this one she cared about and he seemed to mind. She hadn't meant to trick him. She was simply born like this. Time's favorite daughter, with a little help from her favorite doctor.

In the morning, they made love again.

"I can't cum. I almost never do," he said and added sadly, "Rape is common in my country."

"Were you raped?"

"I don't remember. Maybe."

She made him cum.

"Witch," he smiled.

They were going to get breakfast, but neither were hungry. There was a feeling of 'this is the end' in the air. They said their goodbyes on Piazza Trilussa. Her eyes were filled with tears. She walked quickly away and after 70 or so paces, turned to see him still standing in the piazza, blowing his nose. He seemed a bit lost.

She had hoped to see him again before he left, but as the hours rolled by, she realized it was not going to happen. She felt like she'd been hit with a love bat. It was the best date she'd had in a very long time. They made each other feel safe and laugh and cry and cum and dance and hum. What else was there? She determined to go visit him in his country. Turkey was perhaps not the safest place for Americans but at that moment, she would have gone anywhere to be with him.

On the phone, he sounded disinterested when she suggested coming to see him in Istanbul. She hung up disappointed, if not gutted. He did not feel the same for her. Later, she got a message saying he wanted to see her one last time. They met at Piazza Trilussa. He was very late and again she betrayed her recent promises to herself and waited. Finally he showed, sweating like a beast.

"My phone died and I went to the wrong bridge." He seemed sincerely worried he wouldn't find her.

But he looked, acted and sounded like a totally different person to her. Bland, with just a touch of Harry Potter lent to him by his round spectacles. As they walked, it became clear that the man she'd fallen in love with simply did not exist, not really. He was a figment of drugged imagination, both hers and his.

"I choose a safe life," said Ediz. "I am the lonely guy. I meet a woman, have two dates, then I disappear."

"I'm too good for you," she told him in a moment of petulance. But it did not take the sting away much.

"I know," he said kindly and then added, "I cried today, tears of joy. I'd had such a date."

"I should not have told you my age."

"That has nothing to do with it! This is how I am."

But she wasn't sure if she believed it. In fact, she didn't.

They parted ways and she messaged Arash immediately. She did not want to be alone this night. This one hurt.

"I'm jealous, not of those before me, but the one that comes after me," said Arash.

He did all the same things as before, but things were different now. Still he was a gentle soul, and their affection for each other, while not terribly deep, was at least tender and real. She nestled into his wiry, curly hair and slept safely.

- - - - - - - - - - - - - - - - - -

RULE #92 When you date someone on drugs, either them or you, you might have a great time. But it is only a temporary reality.

- - - - - - - - - - - - - - - - - -

To have the perfect date only to discover the man she had it with was a chemical fabrication, well, she knew now how fragile sanity and reality could be.

CHAPTER 60

BELIEVE NOTHING

A night of nightmares was followed by a day of sickness and rebellion. Of feeling abandoned. And then it was all so very clear. Artemisia had set it up so that everyone would leave her so that she could replay this episode over and over and over again. Living in a tourist area, meeting those who were passing through, she got to re-live the time, the place and the emotions of her father leaving. Oh, so cliché, but to the person going through it, always a startling revelation. She spent the next day admitting to her friends, 'I have abandonment issues' with a joke or an apology, or both. She focused. She read the tarot. More of the same. Knowing is not the same as conquering. Perhaps she should just learn to enjoy the ride.

There had been no men in her bed since Arash and no hope for love since Ediz, just a feeling of profound calm. She laughed as she realized that is usually what happened right before a major disaster.

She was the unsinkable Artemisia…she'd ride this wild elephant. That was why she never cared for adventure sports. Her life already was an adventure sport. When you are a single mother on the autism spectrum, walking into a fucking school lobby is an adventure sport, full of unpredictable curves, sights, sounds, sensations. Afterward you just wanted a cold beer and a warm bed. But these days, well she'd seen and done so much the sensations were dulled a bit. The only thing that really excited her now, was uncovering, discovering, excavating, relishing a truth. To make another person see the beauty in themselves that they were unaware of, or the darkness that was stopping them from living.

The calm stayed with her. She cooked, walked, ate alone, played, worked alone. She practiced in the carriage house her landlady had given her the keys to. Because of the heat wave it was downright dangerous to stay in her tiny flat with no air conditioner. And then, there it was.

"Hi."

"*Buongiorno*," she replied.

Almost immediately he told her what date he was coming back and where his hotel was. It was like he'd forgotten they'd parted acerbically or maybe he had her mixed up with someone else.

And then it all made sense. She was here to meet him. The Indian Prince. Ekimet.

They Skyped. He was lying back on his pillow, so gentle, so handsome, such a lovely voice, a smile. It was easy talking to him. She laughed too much, smiled too much.

"Soon you will be in my arms. I will make love to you morning, noon and night but we will see Rome also. I will buy two tickets to everything. I want us to do everything together. Be prepared to do a lot of walking."

Last time they spoke, he was a baby trying to be a wildchild. But it was not his style. He was looking for love, for a home. Or, was he just another scoundrel? *Let's find out*, she thought.

The next day, Google maps was wrong and her tram ended at Piazza Venezia, the worst place in the world to be trying to get somewhere in a hurry. She scurried along in the thin band of shade and boarded a bus, which she disembarked at the next stop because it was a hot smelly sardine can.

When she finally got to his hotel, she was disallowed from going to his room because she did not have a passport. So she waited in the lobby. He arrived after a few minutes, wearing thick sweat pants despite the heat wave, and a less than enthusiastic expression.

"How do I look to you?" she asked.

"You look okay," said Ekimet flatly.

The day was marked by stops and starts, affections and coldness, a wanting to join and a longing to flee on his part.

He did not buy two of everything and told her "I have to do some things alone. It's why I'm here…alone."

It turned out he was in Europe nursing his broken heart. After a month of broken promises, Artemisia had two new mottos. The first: *The future was just the past, dressed up as something different.* The second: *Step up or fuck off.* Somehow her professional life as a consultant had trickled into her personal one.

. . . .

RULE #93 It is not your job to be the bridge between a broken man and his future happiness.

. . . .

It was not her fault she didn't impress Ekimet. If even the view of Rome laid out below his feet did not make a mark, then what chance did she have?

As they walked down the hill to part ways, she said, "You know, I don't have the capacity not to believe someone when they tell me something. You shouldn't have made those promises."

"Believe nothing and no one, not even yourself."

He fell off the curb. She laughed despite herself. It made up for the embarrassment of having put her dress on inside out and having to do a quick change behind a shrub.

"I have great instincts," she countered. "They become overruled by the things people say. I have to believe everything or nothing. No matter how wise I get, how mature, this will never change." She had seen through him weeks ago. It was her desire for love that made her ignore what she knew.

"Then believe nothing. That would be wisest."

He left her at her door, wearing her pretty dress, at 8PM on a date night.

"I miss you" he wrote, minutes later.

Apparently Ekimet didn't realize that goodbye meant goodbye. Perhaps he thought tomorrow was another day. But no, there would be no second chances.

Athena, she shouted silently from her balcony, *Give me a complete person, or as complete as possible and send that one in my path*…instead of these broken pieces that wanted her to fix, reassemble and glue them back together.

From now on, her happiness was as important as anyone's. It was intact, and only in the presence of others, was it subtracted from so violently.

She got no sleep that night. All the broken promises replayed in her mind, all the lies, all the innocent wrongdoing. There was no bitterness, no recrimination, just an empty, windswept beach, a lone palm tree swaying, breakers rolling, the beige of an abandoned holiday camp. That was all that was left of her spirit. Not even the dramatic darkness of a decrepit mine or the strange angles of an old graveyard, just a beige beach. It was time for a change but what sort of change? She could not see a way forward. She could not go back, sideways or up. She could only go inward.

. . . .

RULE #94 The death of a date is usually exposed in the first few minutes.

. . . .

Ediz confessed he had dinner and a liter of wine *before* meeting her. Ekimet revealed that he did not buy "two of everything" as promised, but instead got himself a Roma pass which ensured that she would have to wait in line to buy tickets and feel like she was slowing him down. But she always gave them the benefit of the doubt. After all, she'd put on the pretty dress, the makeup, looked forward to it all day. And often she'd end up having a very good time. It was the disappointment after that she couldn't deal with. Whether they didn't want her, or she didn't want them.

. . . .

RULE #95 If it feels like a mindfuck, it is a mindfuck.

. . . .

There's no debate. It doesn't mean that the person was bad, just bad for you. If they are indecisive, or they were too idealistic, if they misrepresented themselves out of hopefulness for the future, that was their mistake. All Artemisia could do was promise herself never to let that happen again. It had happened too many times, before and after Rasputin.

They were like two bookends now. Rasputin started her on this journey…had Ekimet ended it? She hadn't had the heart to go on any dates since they met. She was back where she started, walking the streets alone, not looking anyone in the eye. Men leered, women sneered, sometimes people even jeered—she realized with jaded amusement how those words rhymed.

She had dated some beautiful men. The thing was,

. . . .

RULE #96 Dating beautiful men didn't make you feel more beautiful. To walk down the street with someone who is busy looking at his own reflection in windows or in other women's eyes only left you feeling depleted.

. . . .

Many men had subtracted from her, few had added.

. . . .

RULE #97 Feeling like you are not being appreciated is not a call to rise to a challenge. In dating, it is a signal to walk away.

. . . .

Quickly, before you become emotionally invested in a situation that could not possibly come to anything but a bad end.

Beauty was everywhere in the world, especially in Rome, but like statues in a museum, was often nothing more than a cold display of ego. Tenderness and character, those were the things that mattered and if a nice pair of pecs came along with it, well that was a bonus.

Finally the hot spell had broken and so had her malaise, her ennui, her dream state. She ran up the hill to her fountain. Rasputin was still there, fooling everyone with his innocent expression. The view of Rome was there, unchanging for decades, centuries, parts of it, for millennia.

She silently shouted over the rooftops and all the way over the Ionian Sea to Athena:

"Who do I belong to?"

"No one and everyone," came the silent answer.

"Where do I belong?"

"Nowhere and everywhere."

If she wanted to pursue love any further, or let it pursue her, at least now she had a rule book tucked under her arm to protect her.

She wanted to escape Rome *now*, but hadn't the faintest idea where to go. Luckily she had business in Athens. *Commitments might be the only things that can really save us*, she thought.

Artemisia finally learned what many five-year-olds know:

. . . .

RULE #98 Not everyone deserved her trust or her love. It had to be *earned* and *proven* over time.

. . . .

It was going to take some real effort to recalibrate. But she was quite certain she could do it.

CHAPTER 61

(ALMOST) FINAL THOUGHTS

So here I am, Artemisia.

After I left Rome, I went to Athens and performed a play which I wrote and scored. Only this newfound self-confidence and knowledge could have made this possible. There I made new friends, forged deeper connections with old ones; I've found new paramours and stayed connected with some I'd met on this journey. I am finally free because I know I have options, we all do, no matter what the situation, no matter how dark, how lonely. I had been at times, so deep in a dark well that I felt I really touched hell. And now, finally, nothing gets me down for long. I've become happier and stronger than I ever thought possible. Some people and some ideas had to be let go to make that happen. I had to learn:

RULE #99 In the search for love and romance, one has to put oneself first.

This is contrary to what so many of us have been taught, i.e. to find someone to serve. But whether or not they are worthy of that takes time to discover. Of course when you have children, their needs *are* part of your needs.

On one of my last days in Athens, a young man behind the counter of a café bar said "I have worked here six years and you have the most beautiful eyes I have seen this whole time."

I looked up abruptly into a pair of sincere naive ones, so like mine used to be. In a year of emotionless sex and ordinary come-on lines, a few things stood out like little beacons. This young man's sweet words were one of them, and just what I needed at the time.

. . . .

RULE #100 A good compliment does not make a woman or man feel cheap. It lingers like a haunting refrain and makes the receiver and the giver feel elevated.

. . . .

Although I brooded that my adventure did not have the happy ending I had sought, in many ways, it does. I went back in NY where I devoted myself to family and will do so every year for three months. The rest of the time I will spend elsewhere, devoted to my art, career, friends, love life, and whatever else the world has yet to offer. And they finally understand, that some women are made for home and hearth and others are dragons, sailing the skies looking to make their mark on the wider world. And there are a billion options in between.

The happiest conclusion of all, is that I am done with the kind of relationship that promises much, but delivers only heartache and pain, that sucks in everything good and light, like a black hole. As I look back, I've learned so much I barely recognize the woman in chapter one.

And now, I'd like to leave you with a few last rules, things that didn't seem to fit in anywhere exactly, but are worth telling.

RULE #101 Never, *ever* pine for a man that doesn't want you.

It takes willpower but everyone has some.

RULE #102 Don't waste your life and time believing in romantic comedies.

I used to love them, but they create unrealistic expectations in a literal naive mind. Some of us waited patiently for Hugh Grant, Hugh Jackman—any Hugh would do. As long as he was sexy, intelligent, kind, fit, financially solvent if not rich, you know, the kind of man that comes along every day.

RULE #103 If you love someone and they are all you can think about, all you desire, but they don't want you, it's not love, it's obsession.

To cure an obsession, we have to spread our attention around, share it among many things, whether it's books, music, movies or people. If you obsess over one man or woman, date others, whether you want to or not. Eventually you will see that the original one made you unhappy. Maybe not with their presence but with their *absence*. And that speaks volumes.

. . . .

RULE #104 Don't call anyone a cougar or MYLF, or let anyone call you either of those. It's rude, sexist and ageist and says much more about the one saying it, than the one they're saying it about.

. . . .

If we are talking about people who go after underage victims, they are criminals and predators. There's no cutesy term for that.

. . . .

RULE #105 You don't 'fuck' a single mother. You love her or you get out of the way.

. . . .

A lot of my misadventures started as the result of being played by a man years ago when I was just looking to create a happy home for my young daughter. Ladies, men will see this longing, this vacancy, and use it to their advantage. Protect yourselves and your children. They are the ones that will always love you, if you treat them well. They are the ones that matter.

. . . .

RULE #106 No means no. The absence of yes also means no. Nothing turns me off more than being pressured into sex. If any gentlemen are reading this book, most women do like sex, so if they're saying no, it means they really don't want it. Maybe they really don't want it with you, maybe they really don't want it at that time. It doesn't matter, that's not your business. It's her business; it's our business.

. . . .

CHAPTER 62

SAFE SEX IS THE BEST SEX

I alluded to safety throughout this story, but truly I was inconsistent in my own self-protection, and indeed, that of my partners. I was extremely fortunate that nothing went wrong in that regard. Some of you may already be vigilantly self-protective, others more devil-may-care. As I learned, as I changed, I became much more consistent in my safe sex practices. As I stated in the Introduction, *This is not, by any means, a how-to book.* It is much more like a how not to. Hear my voice in your head if and when you start to forget that. I put myself in great mental, physical and spiritual danger to help those even less savvy than myself, so that they would be wiser and safer than I was. As I look back on the girl and then the woman I was, I want to shout through time and space, *Love yourself, protect yourself, put yourself first.* But I was raised in a time and in a culture that almost demanded women be victims in romance and that they should always put men's needs first.

I'd suggest going through the book and listing the rules—especially the ones about safety—yourself, it will help them stay in your mind when you need them most.

Men (and women) were always telling me "Be quiet, you're weird, there's something wrong with you, shut up, go away, you don't deserve to be treated with respect." I was a natural born feminist, and I was made to feel like a freak for it. I saw the Employment Rights Act vetoed, I saw women running for office lose time and again. I saw the most misogynistic men being elected. I saw film after film being made about some macho guy, and the woman was always there for him to talk to about himself...always the same old boring story in a million variations.

Women are the most interesting creatures, we have the best stories, and we are oh so very capable at virtually anything we put our minds to. Never let Aspergers, your gender, or anything else, stick you in the armchair by the fire. We have to fight a little bit longer to have top billing. Women have to be fierce. And I'm proud to say, I'm seeing it happen all around me now—women both on and off the spectrum, speaking up, taking their place, demanding respect. (You can't command it from a sexist—you have to demand it.)

As for love, I am still a big fan. Despite everything, my light still glows. The book is closed, but not the story. Write yours with passion.

Love, Artemisia